How to Play Golf

2011 Edition

Reprinted and Republished By Library Tales Publishing
www.librarytalespublishing.com

Edited By Sharon Ross

Copyright © 2009-2010 by Library Tales Publishing.
Library Tales Publishing, New York, NY, 10001

ISBN: 978-145652757-0

Printed in the United States of America

HOW TO PLAY GOLF

Originally Written By H. J. Whigham in 1897

REPUBLISHED AND PRINTED
BY
LIBRARY TALES PUBLISHING

To

CHARLES BLAIR MACDONALD

Who has done more than anyone else to promote the best interests of golf in America, this volume is dedicated.

The author begs to acknowledge his indebtedness to Mr. E. Burton Holmes for the use of the pictures illustrating this volume.

Contents

CHAPTER I
ADVICE TO BEGINNERS

The term beginner, as applied to the game of golf, covers a multitude of varying aims and aspirations; and since advice is surely wasted upon those who either do not need it or have no desire for it, we may, for economical purposes, classify beginners under three heads, and state directly the particular kind of novice to whom the following suggestions are offered.

The first class, then, is composed of boys under the age of discretion, who learn games by a natural process of imitation and assimilation; in the second are found all those of dyspeptic habits who have been ordered by their physicians to take a round of golf, either as a tonic or a counter irritant; the third, and by far the largest, class includes men and women of all ages and temperaments, who by accident or intention, have taken an interest in the game sufficient to inspire them with a desire for improvement, and yet find a difficulty in acquiring any accuracy of form or execution on account of the lack of practical information upon the subject.

Professional Teaching

It is to this last and most sympathetic class that I desire chiefly to address a few remarks, with just a word of explanation in advance. Many may object to the presumption that information really is lacking. There are standard works upon the science of golf, and every links in America, or indeed in any other well regulated community, is provided with a first class professional direct from the royal and ancient home of the game in Scotland. And yet the Badminton book in its general tone is, like all scientific works, more an aid to experts than a consolation to beginners who have been led astray in their youth by devotion to baseball or cricket. As for the professional, the disadvantages under which he imparts his instruction must be taken into consideration before his advice can be accepted with absolute faith.

Generally speaking, he is young, and without experience in the matter of teaching. He is ignorant of the ways of the people he has to deal with, and having no respect for any game but his own, he is unable to distinguish between errors which come from innate viciousness and those which have been induced by familiarity with the bat or the racket. Lastly, he can seldom account for his own proficiency.

Golf with him is more a second nature than an accomplishment; he succeeds in his art not of malice prepense, as Aristotle would say, but simply because he cannot help it; and the fact that he is a good player is no criterion whatever of his ability as an instructor of others.

Of course there are many professionals who are excellent teachers. But I have seen so many novices, both in America and England, who, in spite of professional coaching or because of it are attempting to play golf in a manner that never can be anything but a source of grief to themselves and pity in their friends, that I have determined to lay down a few simple maxims which are not based upon any dogma or theory, but upon actual observation.

The Choice of Weapon

Let us begin at the very beginning, then, and having taken it for granted that the tyro really wishes to play golf, and not some other inferior game, let us put him in the right direction at the start.

He must not, in the first place, buy a complete set of clubs, because he cannot possibly expect to play with more than three of them under two months' time, and the rest will only distract his attention.

Score Counting must be Avoided

Secondly, he will be wise to keep off the regular course as long as possible, for as soon as he plays eighteen holes he will begin to count his score and trouble the handicapper. This is the most prevalent disease among young golfers, and one that will check his progress more than anything else. I may be pardoned, therefore, for dwelling a moment upon the subject. The average beginner finds it very difficult to understand why he should be warned against this score counting habit, arguing, with some show of plausibility that the lowering of one's record is a strong incentive toward improvement in the game.

He forgets, however, that apart from the fact that his endeavors to get below the hundred will make him unfit for human companionship, the mere anxiety to succeed in a nominal and numerical way must have a bad effect upon his style. He will adopt any and every method whereby he may the more readily reach the hole; some friend will give him a piece of advice which will make him more accurate for the time being, but will sacrifice for him all hopes of ever hitting the ball in the right way; so that, finally, by the time he has surprised himself by going the whole round of eighteen holes in ninety nine strokes, without a single effort of the imagination, and has won several useless and inartistic cups, he will find that he has forfeited all possibility of becoming a first class player.

It would be a good rule, then, for every beginner to refuse to count his score until he has played six months; and above all let him remember that it is better to miss the ball fifty times in succession in the right way than to hit it once by some inauthentic trick.

* Prior to the 17th century balls were made of wood or wool in a leather cover. After the 17th century feathers were boiled and compressed, then sewn in a leather cover. It continued to evolve to a solid gutta percha (or a mixture with gutta percha other substances) in the 1850's and strip rubber wound around a core in the 1900's. Presently made of solid compressed synthetic rubber with hundreds of surface indentations which aid in the flight of the ball.

Use a Wooden Club

It will be best for our novice to retire with his caddy or his adviser to some remote locality with plenty of old balls and only one club. That club must be of the wooden variety. The shaft should be strong, but not too clumsy, with just a little spring at the lower end. The head should be a bulger.

It is a mystery to me why every beginner is taught to play with an old fashioned, long headed driver. It would be just as sensible to offer a young tennis player one of the old lob sided rackets to learn the game with. The bulger is not only the best kind of head for experts, but it was especially invented to obviate the faults which are most inherent in young players. The compact form of the head makes accurate hitting far more easily, and the bulge is intended to counteract all tendencies to slice and pull.

The angle of the head with the shaft should not be too obtuse. Tastes vary, of course, on that point, but the general fault in wooden clubs is that they err in not being sufficiently upright.

* Spring is the flexibility of the club shaft.

** A wood is a club, which can be made of wood or metal, that has a large head and is used for shots requiring greater distance. Usually a numbered set of 5 or more starting with the driver and proceeding to the 5 wood

The Position of the Hands

The club having been selected, attention should be given to the grip. There are only two possible positions for the hands in driving, and they are shown on the next page. The position of the left hand is the same in both cases. The shaft of the club must be gripped firmly in the palm in such a way that when the ball is addressed, the fingers, with the exception of the *third* joint of the *first* finger and the *second* joint of the thumb, are invisible. There is no other way of holding the club in the left hand. And yet I have seen numbers of beginners who have been coached for weeks, holding the left hand underneath the club to such an extent that the first and second joints of the fingers are plainly visible above the shaft. The most casual trial will prove that the latter method is quite incompatible with an easy swing.

With regard to the right hand, there are two opinions among the experts. Generally speaking, the best players hold the club lightly, but not loosely, in the fingers of the right hand in such a manner that the thumb lies across the upper surface of the shaft, with the first joints of the fingers barely visible. This has always been the accepted book form, and the beginner will probably find it wise to adopt it, unless the second way is distinctly easier for him.

POSITION OF THE HANDS

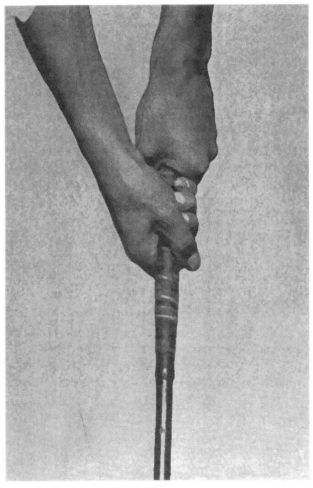

WITH THE CLUB IN THE FINGERS OF THE RIGHT HAND

In the second illustration it will be observed that the club is grasped firmly in the palm of the right hand, and the hand is held under the shaft, so that the second joints of the fingers are clearly visible above it.

Although I should favor the first position, there can be no doubt that the second way has been made enormously effective in the hands of many of the best players, both professional and amateur. It is a marked peculiarity of the St. Andrews players, who probably learned it from the Kirkcaldy brothers; but it is certainly not confined to St. Andrews. Mr. John Ball, Jr., to mention no others, holds the club tightly in the palm of the right hand; and if the poll could be taken, it would be very hard to say upon which side the majority of first class golfers would be found. Two of the finest drivers in Scotland, Mr. Edward Blackwell and Mr. F. G. Tait, certainly incline to the second method, and yet the first is invariably recommended in books.

* Amateur is a golfer who plays without monetary compensation.

** The Royal and Ancient Golf Club of St Andrews is one of the oldest and most prestigious golf clubs in the world (the oldest being the Honourable Company of Edinburgh Golfers at Muirfield). It is based in St Andrews, Fife, Scotland, and is regarded as the worldwide "Home of Golf". Formerly, it was also one of the governing authorities of the game, but in 2004 this role was handed over to a newly formed group of companies, collectively known as The R&A.

POSITION OF THE HANDS

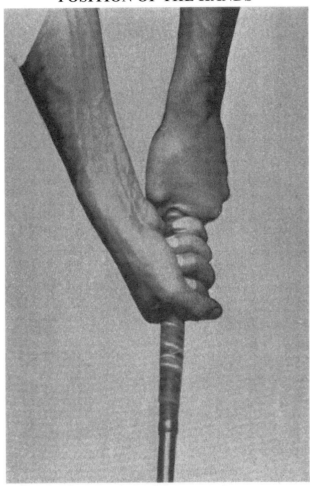

WITH THE CLUB IN THE PALM OF THE RIGHT HAND

The books and the professional advisers can hardly do otherwise, however, because one of their first maxims is that the club must be held loosely in the right hand. Now, it is plain it cannot be held very loosely in the second way. The fact is that the old maxim, which is thrown at the head of every beginner, is responsible for an untold multitude of misfortunes. I would rather say, hold firmly with both hands and choose whichever method pleases you best, only remembering this that the first admits of an easier and rather more graceful swing, while the second enables the player to employ the whole force of the right forearm and that is the secret of most long driving. At present, however, we have nothing to do with long driving. We shall be very well content if the ball is struck clean, irrespective of the distance.

The Stance

Let the novice grasp his club in one of the manners described, and stand square to the ball, not stooping too much, nor yet uncompromisingly rigid. The books tell him that he may stand, as regards the ball, in one of two ways, basing their arguments upon the best form. But driving from the left leg has gone out so much in the last few years that the open style may be regarded as the only one which it is worthwhile to teach beginners.

THE STANCE

POSITION IN DRIVING

He must take his position, then, with the ball placed rather more toward his left than his right leg, and at such a distance that he can place the head of the club comfortably behind it without stooping or stretching out the arms, and leaving as obtuse an angle as possible between the arms and the shaft of the club.

The feet should be from two to two and a half feet apart, according to height, and the right if anything advanced a trifle in front of the left. This style has generally been referred to as driving off the right leg, as opposed to the method of driving from the left leg, already mentioned. But that is in reality an abuse of language.

When the right leg is advanced so far that the weight of the body rests almost entirely upon it, the expression is perfectly correct; but that is not what is at present intended. The beginner must accustom himself to stand fairly erect, with the weight of the body equally distributed between each leg; he will then drive not from one or the other, but from both, and that is the only correct method.

In swinging back he will let the weight fall naturally upon the right foot until the top of the swing is reached. In coming forward again, the weight will follow the club, and when the drive is finished it will rest almost entirely upon the left foot. But this must be done unconsciously. As soon as the beginner allows himself to think about changing his center of gravity his swing is sure to get out of gear. It will be quite sufficient; then, if he will stand correctly in the first place, and swing as I shall instruct him.

The Swing

Here is the crucial point. He will probably be persuaded to imitate the long swing of his professional adviser. If he does so, he is almost certainly lost. There are exceptions even to this rule, but generally speaking, no man or woman whose muscles have become set, should ever attempt a full swing until it comes of its own accord.

Begin with what your professional calls a half-shot. That is to say, let the arms go back just as far as possible without making a break in the motion. The club must swing backward and forward as smoothly as the pendulum of a clock. The left wrist and elbow should be kept almost in a straight line, and only the right wrist and elbow should be bent as the club moves backward. Practice this stroke until you can hit the ball accurately, and you will be astonished how far it will go with only a very small expenditure of force.

Your young golfer, however, is a very ambitious individual, and he will not be content to forego his cherished St. Andrews swing unless he is given good reasons. He will generally argue that form must be acquired at any cost, and confront me with my own statement that it is better to miss the ball in the right way than to hit it in the wrong. First, then, let me ask him whether it is not far better to achieve a half swing than no swing at all.

He must remember that driving is entirely a matter of swing. As soon as he begins to hit *at* the ball he is hopelessly ruined. He must at all costs learn to sweep the ball away as if it were an object of no weight at all. Consequently, if he can learn a true half swing, he is at least on the road to grace; whereas the contortions which he goes through in acquiring what he imagines to be the proper St. Andrews style do not constitute a swing at all, and he will probably spend months and months attempting to sandpaper it down into something like a regular sweep.

In the meantime his less ambitious brother in golf will have outstripped him with ease; not, be it understood, in the matter of score for that is of no importance but in the effectiveness of his play and the evenness of his swing.

Of course it is not intended that the late beginner should not in time develop a real St. Andrews swing. The only question is: How can he do it most easily? When he has played long enough and watched the motions of all the first class golfers he may come across, he will gradually find his swing lengthening out without any conscious effort on his own part and without any break in the motion.

A golfing swing is rather like the human voice. There is a definite break which years of practice only can smooth away. In training the voice the teacher develops both the lower and the upper register, and in so doing works one into the other so as to conceal the break.

The teacher in golf - at least, where he has to deal with adult pupils - should adopt just the contrary method. He should develop the lower register only, and go on extending it until it gradually glides into the upper register without encountering the break at all. That is the theoretical reason for encouraging the half swing. Fortunately, in this case the practice bears out the theory. At the present moment three of the best American players, according to public form, are A. H. Fenn, A. Tyng and H. Harriman.

There are several younger players who are quite as good now, and probably will very soon pass the older contingent in the race. But these college boys, like Betts, Reid, Terry, Walter Smith, Bayard and many others, hardly enter into the present discussion. They have learned the game early enough in life to imitate the regular professional swing without danger.

Of the older golfers, however, Fenn and Tyng have certainly earned the right to be considered in the front rank, and Harriman I class with them, not because his record is so extensive, nor because he happened to defeat Tyng in playing for the amateur championship, but because his style strikes me as being the best exposition of the method which ought to be followed by adult beginners.

Turn to the photographs of these players, and you will observe that not one of them has a full swing, Fenn and Tyng being most remarkable in this respect. But you will also see that in each case the stroke is followed through to the finish. Thus the head of the club is kept traveling as long as possible in the line of the ball's flight. Another point will strike you if you look carefully at the different illustrations: You will see that in Harriman's case the hands go back very nearly as far as in the pictures of the Scotch players. And yet the casual observer would never suspect Harriman of having a full swing; which goes to prove that the eye is often deceived, and that what looks like a very long swing is in reality not so very much longer than the stroke which I recommend to the beginner.

The argument, moreover, does not apply to American players alone. In the first rank of English and Scotch golfers it would be hard to find a single expert who did not learn the game as a boy. But among those who began later in life, the best are certainly those who use little more than a half swing. Two good instances come readily to mind: Mr. Oswald, who was last year captain of the St. Andrews golf club, is one of the steadiest players on any links. He is not absolutely first class, but there are very few players who can give him odds with safety; yet in driving, his hands hardly reach the level of his shoulder.

Mr. Walter De Zoete is another and even more extraordinary case in point. He plays with an easy half swing, and he has passed the age when men expect to be preeminent in sports; yet there is hardly a golfer, young or old, who can beat him over his native heath at North Berwick in Scotland.

The Finish of the Stroke

I hope, then, that the advantages of the short swing for those who begin golf comparatively late in life are by this time sufficiently apparent. Having adopted this method, the beginner must remember that the finish of the stroke is at least as important as the beginning. It is absolutely necessary that he should keep the head of the club traveling in the line of the ball's flight as long as possible, and this can only be done by letting the weight of the body follow the stroke until it rests entirely on the left leg. The right shoulder must also come forward, and the tendency to draw back both the shoulders and the arms after the ball has been struck must be overcome at any price. Examine the different positions at the end of the stroke, and you will see that there is more of the swing after the ball is hit than before; the practical explanation of which is that in order to secure a good finish the club must be traveling very fast when it reaches the ball. If, on the other hand, the stroke is ended as soon as the ball is struck the swing must be gradually becoming slower before the club reaches the ball, and the drive is robbed of most of its force.

In actual practice you will find that as the club goes back the heel of the left foot is torn, as it were, from the ground. Similarly, when the stroke is finished, if the weight is carried through correctly, the right heel is sure to rise. But in both cases the action must be unconscious. Do not pay any attention to a professional adviser who tells you to turn your heel.

There is absolutely no virtue in the motion unless it is spontaneous. Practice your swing constantly and the rest will come in due time.

Summary

To put it shortly and negatively, then:

1. *Don't begin by counting your score.*

2. *Don't use an iron club, nor an old fashioned wooden one.*

3. *Don't hold loosely with your right hand.*

4. *Don't raise either heel from the ground until it comes naturally.*

Don't, above all, as you value your golfing future, adopt a full St. Andrews swing. So much in the way of suggestion to the real beginner; In the next chapter I shall address a few remarks to those who have advanced far enough to play a definite kind of game, whether good, bad or indifferent.

Driving - American Style

Mr. W. R. Betts

Mr. A. H. Fenn

Mr. J. A. Tyng

Mr. H. M. Harriman

MR. W. R. BETTS
YALE GOLF CLUB

I. At the Top of the Swing

II. Coming Through

III. The Finish

I

III

MR. A. H. FRNN
PALMETTO GOLF CLUB

I. At the Top of the Swing

II. Coming Through

III. The Finish

I

II

CHAPTER II
THE LONG GAME

The young golfer who has learned with some difficulty to play a moderately steady game is certain to experience relapses from time to time, and it is the object of the present chapter to point out the most fruitful sources of error in driving from the tee and through the green.

Faults to be Avoided

When he is alternately hitting his ball on the top, and striking the ground several inches behind it, he will probably be told that he is pressing or taking his eye off the ball. But neither of these reasons is sufficient to explain consistent bad play.

The most frequent fault which assails all golfers, both good and bad, consists in standing too much in front of the ball. That is to say, the ball is placed opposite the right foot, instead of being very nearly opposite the left. The consequence is that the club comes down upon the top of the ball or behind it, as the case may be, instead of meeting it just as the head is on the rise. The effect on the swing itself is extremely detrimental, for not only does the player strike the ball at the wrong point of the circle, but he begins to chop down upon it instead of sweeping it away. Whenever, therefore, you find yourself hitting your ball on the top or else getting it very high in the air, examine carefully your position, and you will generally find that your ball is too near your right foot.

Another fault which manifests itself in various ways consists in falling back at the end of the stroke. The arms and shoulders, instead of following the line of the ball's flight, are drawn quickly round to the left, and the consequence is a terrific pull; or else the ball is struck on the toe of the club and flies off to the right. The effect in both cases is disastrous, and the two shots are so entirely unlike that the novice does not recognize the fact that both are caused by the same error in style. Very often, too, the driving is loose and fails in the matter of distance because the player is not standing up squarely to the ball. His hands are getting too low, the angle between the arms and the shaft is too pronounced, and the sole of the club is not placed evenly on the ground when the ball is addressed. Very often, too, the club is being held too loosely, the thumbs are straying down the shaft instead of across it, and the club is allowed to turn as it strikes the ball.

All these errors, however slight, will have a bad effect upon the flight of the ball. So that generally speaking, when a player is driving poorly, he ought to brace himself up, take a firmer grip of his club, stand more erect, and be sure that he is soling the head of his club squarely behind the ball, so that both toe and heel are on the ground, and the surface of the face makes a right angle with the surface of the earth.

In attempting this cure, he may perhaps go to the other extreme and become almost rigid. But that is the better fault of the two. It is only when a man is at the very top of his game; when eye and hand are in exact accord, that he can with safety loosen every muscle in his body in order to get every ounce of weight into the swing. When a player gets to this state he is a long way beyond advice. He can hold his club with the very lightest grip, he can swing rapidly and with all his might, and it does not matter very much whether he looks at the ball or not.

This is a state of things, however, which rarely comes to anyone except the first class player. The average golfer must be content for the most part to purchase accuracy at the expense of a little flexibility. After all, driving is mainly a matter of following the stroke through with the arms and shoulders, and for that reason the half swing should be continually practiced, because there a man is bound to follow through in order to get any distance at all; so that when you are driving short or slicing badly, go back to a half swing for an hour or two and learn to get the arms and shoulders well away after the ball.

The Refinement of Driving

The rules for driving off the tee and brassey play are rather similar to the rules for the fourth hand at whist. All you have got to do is to hit the ball. But there are a few refinements which may be brought into play with a little practice.

Allowing for Wind

A great many golfers who have risen well into the second rank, find that their game deteriorates tremendously in a high wind. Even the best players are often disturbed by the elements, and it seems to me that their difficulty arises from a very simple and very common fault.

In golf, as in archery, the man who stands most firmly on his feet will always, other things being equal, beat his opponents on a stormy day. It is obvious, therefore, that the higher the wind the more easily must the player swing his club; otherwise he is bound to lose his balance. Yet the constant tendency is to use an extra effort, especially in playing against the wind. Remember, then, the swing must be particularly easy, and special attention must be given to the follow through - your object being to hit the ball absolutely clean. On a calm day a ball may be sliced or pulled or hit high in the air, without great loss of distance. On a windy day, the slightest inaccuracy is ten times exaggerated, and the man who is accustomed to drive with a cut will find himself hopelessly out of the running.

Consequently, your first care on a windy day must be to swing absolutely true, and this is impossible if any attempt is made to force the stroke.

Secondly, do not try to drive a low ball against the wind. It is no uncommon thing to hear even a first class player excusing himself for a very bad shot, by explaining that he was trying to half top the ball, so as to keep it near the ground in its flight. He ought to know r that, wind or no wind, a ball that is half topped will not fly so far as one that is clean hit. Moreover, in placing your ball in such a position as to hit it half on the top, you are almost certainly interfering with your swing, and the result may either be a ball that runs along the ground into the nearest bunker, or one that spouts into the air and is instantly checked by the wind.

Remember that a really clean hit ball from a low tee never flies very high, and the cleaner it is struck the better will it keep its course, even in the teeth of a gale.

In driving against the wind, therefore, it is sufficient to bear in mind that you must swing easily and in your natural way. Any extra effort of any sort will assuredly prove disastrous.

Similarly, with a strong wind behind you, do not try to drive an abnormally long ball. If you do, you will probably lose your balance and fail to hit the ball clean, in which case all the advantage of the wind is lost.

Driving with a Cross Wind

A wind that blows across the course is rather more difficult to deal with. Under such circumstances a ball that is driven absolutely straight will suffer a certain hindrance. You may, however, make such a use of the wind. That it actually helps rather than impedes your stroke. Technically speaking, you can play for a pull with the wind blowing from right to left, and play for a slice with the wind blowing from left to right.

These terms are a little misleading, because in reality you must pull or slice, as the case may be, only to a fraction of a hair's breadth. It is easy enough to pull your ball badly. You need only stand in front of it, aim well to the right, and the pull will come. But then you will find that your ball travels no farther than if you had hit it straight down the course. The proper method is far more artistic. You must aim very slightly to the right, place your ball a very little farther back than usual, grip your club firmly in both hands, and then hit your ball straight and clean, without thinking of the pull at all. As soon as you begin to think about it, you will draw your arms and shoulders round to the left at the end of the swing, and the result will be a very bad pull indeed. All you have got to do is to hit the ball true and follow the stroke through to the finish, and the wind will do the rest.

When the wind is in the other direction, you must be particularly careful not to slice, because however much you may allow for it, a slice is almost sure to land you in trouble. And yet it is very hard to avoid slicing with a wind blowing over your left shoulder, because in aiming well to the left you forget to change the position of the ball in addressing it; consequently it is too far back, and a true swing is impossible.

Remember, then, in playing for a slice you must endeavor before all things not to slice at all. Aim to the left and keep the ball well in front of you when you address it that is to say, almost opposite to your left foot.

On Long Driving

Long driving has so many fascinations, especially for the beginner, that any discovery of a royal road toward acquiring the habit would be exceedingly welcome. Unfortunately there is no possibility of any such discovery. Long driving is simply another expression for clean hitting. No man who does not swing true will ever be a long driver. He may occasionally by some accident get the whole weight of his body into the stroke and hit the ball a very great distance, but that will not constitute him a long driver. It is the average that tells and not the one good drive out of ten when the others are all bad. And a true swing can only be acquired by steady practice. At first perhaps only the arms can be brought into play. But by degrees the shoulders and the hips will become suppler.

Examine the accompanying illustrations carefully, and you will see that at the top of the swing every ounce in the body almost rests on the right leg. As the club comes down, the balance is restored and the weight is almost evenly distributed as the ball is struck; but it is moving forward all the time until at the finish of the stroke it rests entirely on the left leg. And yet, although the weight changes, the body does not appear to alter its position to any great extent; the shoulders revolve upon an almost immovable axis. There must be no forward movement of the whole person as there is in baseball or cricket.

The weight certainly moves, and that is where the strength of the stroke comes from, but it must be transferred almost invisibly, and the momentum must be applied to the ball chiefly through the medium of the right shoulder and forearm.

Now, all this may sound very vague, but if you study the illustrations you will understand partly what is meant, and if you will go out and watch a good driver at work you will understand a great deal better. In fact, if you want to succeed in the game you should never miss an opportunity of seeing a really first class player exercising his art; it will do you far better than a thousand verbal lessons.

And then, when you have learned to use your shoulders in the right way, and find that you are really getting the weight of your body into the stroke, you may be able to employ your wrists. There is a certain snap of the wrists which cannot possibly be described, but which nevertheless is the secret of all very long driving. In order to bring it into use, it is necessary that the muscles of the arm should not be taut; and that is equivalent to saying that the player must be at the very top of his game.

Consequently for all practical purposes the wrists may be forgotten in driving. When the time comes to use them, the player will be beyond the reach of advice.

* Driver is the longest-hitting modern wooden club, used primarily from the tee when maximum distance is required. Also called the No. 1 wood. driving range An area or building used for the purpose of practicing tee-shots and other strokes.

Brassey Play

The term brassey play is generally applied to all the strokes made through the green with a wooden club. And yet the less the brassey is used the better it will be, both for the green and the player. Courses are, or should be, kept in such good condition, at the present time that a driver may be used in nearly every case. But many players employ a brassey simply from habit, or because they desire to save a favorite club. A moment's consideration will suffice to show that the brass on the sole of the club is a certain handicap because it alters the balance. Why not employ the old fashioned spoon? In fact, why not duplicate your driver almost exactly, simply shortening the shaft to some slight extent, and perhaps lying back the face a very little? It stands to reason that a man can play more accurately with one club than two, and where he has to employ two; they should be as nearly alike as possible.

Of course, on rough ground, where the lies are hard and cuppy, the brassey is almost a necessity, for no other club will stand the wear and tear. But for a good green it seems more reasonable to employ either a driver or club very similar in weight and lie, the only difference being in the shaft, which for playing through the green should be rather shorter and less supple.

Beyond this there is very little to say about brassey play which has not already been pointed out in discussing the drive from the tee. Only one rule should be insisted upon: the worse the lie, the easier should the swing be; and particularly so in playing a hanging ball.

In the latter case, remember to sole the club squarely on the ground, and not with its face upward. In other words, play the ball as if it was not hanging at all, and the natural curve of flight will raise it sufficiently for all practical purposes. Occasionally, when the ball is hanging and there is a steep face immediately in front, it may be necessary to aim to the left, hit the ball rather on the heel, and allow for the curve. But this is rather a desperate method. In such cases it is generally better to discard the wooden club and use an iron.

* Iron is any one of a number of clubs with a head made of iron or steel. See definitions for individual clubs "two iron" etc. jungle A slang term for heavy rough.

Driving - Scotch Style

Mr. H. J. Whigham

Mr. C. B. Macdonald

Mr. F. S. Douglas

MR. H. J. WHIGHAM
ONWKNTSIA CLUB

CHAPTER III
IRON PLAY

The approach shot in all its various forms is the most difficult and the most important part of the game of golf, and yet it is the stroke which the beginner, as a rule, practices least and attempts most erroneously.

There are two reasons for his shortcomings in this respect. In the first place, he starts at the wrong end. Instead of learning to play a very short approach to begin with, and then going on to extend the capacity of his half stroke, he regards any kind of iron shot as a modification of a full drive, and so attempts to play up to the hole with a flabby and half hearted full swing; whereas, if he did but know it, he could cover the same distance far more easily with a third of the exertion and with far greater accuracy.

In the second place, the tendency to enter handicap competitions at an early stage of his career has the effect of crippling his stroke even more in the approach than in the drive. He is determined to get to the green somehow or other, and so generally purchases an abomination of modern golf, known as a lofter, with which he certainly avoids bunkers, but only at the expense of correct style and future prospects.

Two things, then, must be borne in mind in the beginning. The shorter your swing, the greater your accuracy; and secondly, the less your club is lofted the steadier your game will be. The reason for the latter proposition is very obvious. With a club that is excessively laid back, the slightest error in hitting the ball, either too high or too low, will make an enormous difference in the distance. With a club that is not laid back so far, the ball may be hit high or low, and travel almost the same distance in either case. It is true that most good players use the mashie to a large extent, but you will generally find that the mashie which is used by a good approacher is a very different weapon from the shovel faced lofter which is generally put in the hands of a novice.

Choice of Club

And even the mashie may well be discarded until the use of the light iron has been thoroughly acquired. It is hardly necessary to state that it is advisable, as far as possible, to employ only one club for all the approach shots within a hundred yards of the hole. Occasionally a steep bunker has to be negotiated when the hole lies only a few yards beyond it, and then a mashie is practically a necessity unless you have acquired the art of putting a strong back spin upon the ball. But shots of that nature need not trouble the beginner very seriously. He may be well contented if he can learn in the space of a few months to play a good straightforward approach where he can drop his ball twenty yards short of the hole and let it roll the rest of the way.

Let him take, then, what is known as a light or medium iron, a club which is quite sufficiently laid back for all practical purposes, and leaving the mashie severely alone, let him devote himself for an hour or so each day to playing the approach shot. And in order to avoid any tendency to force the stroke, let him begin at a distance from the hole - say thirty or forty yards - which he can cover with a very small expenditure of force.

Position

In playing this stroke, the stand should be changed from that required in driving. The line of the feet should be at an angle of nearly 45° with the line of the ball's flight, so that the player may face the hole; and the ball should be more nearly opposite the right foot than the left. The player must be careful, however, to give his arms perfectly free play, and on no account must the right elbow rest upon the hip.

The Hands

In gripping the club the player may adopt the same position of the hands as in driving, but it would be better in playing so short an approach as this, if he would relax the grip of the left hand and hold the shaft of the club in the fingers instead of the palm. But if he does so, he must not let the thumbs stray down the shaft of the club, nor must he hold the shaft loosely with either hand. If he does so, he will find that the head of the club is apt to turn ever so little as the ball is struck, and the result is very disastrous.

As for the stroke itself, disabuse your mind entirely of the idea that you are playing a wrist shot. There never was a more misleading term than that which is invariably applied to every shot in golf which does not necessitate a full swing. There are occasions, of course, where a very delicate lofting stroke has to be played, and an expert may in such cases play entirely with his wrists.

But as a general rule, even a short approach of thirty five yards employs the forearm, and even to a certain extent the shoulder. The wrist in reality enters very little into the stroke.

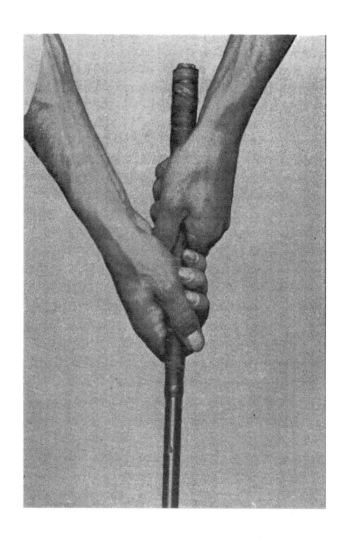

POSITION OF THE HANDS FOR THE SHORT APPROACH

Nothing can be more important than to recognize this truth, for the chief difficulty which most young players experience in learning to approach arises from the fact that they imagine that they must swing with their wrists only, which is in itself a physical impossibility. The stroke must, in reality, be played with the left arm almost straight. As the club goes back the right elbow is bent and the right wrist moves perceptibly. The head of the club should travel very near the ground, and in a straight line backward. In coming forward the left arm is still kept very nearly straight (but not rigid), and after the ball is struck the right arm straightens out to the finish until the player is pointing with arms and club stretched out toward the hole.

Examine very carefully the illustrations of the approach shot at forty yards, and you will see that, in the first place, the arms are free of contact with the body; secondly, the wrists change their position very slightly during the stroke; thirdly, the arms are employed right up to the shoulder; and fourthly, the hands travel a long way after the ball.

Observe, on the other hand, the wrist shot as it is played by nearly every beginner, and you will see that the arms do not work freely because they are not supposed to enter into the stroke, the wrists are bent backward and forward, and the hands are held back at the finish instead of being allowed to follow the flight of the ball. It is the left arm especially that is cramped by this attempt to play with the wrists.

Remember, then, particularly to let the left arm go out after hitting the ball, otherwise the head of the iron is brought round to the left instead of following through.

If you play the stroke in the proper way you will have no difficulty whatever in raising the ball from the ground. Therefore it is quite unnecessary to use a lofter, or even a mashie, unless you are compelled, on account of the proximity of a bunker, to drop the ball very dead. Above all, do not lay the face of your iron back in addressing the ball, thinking thereby to lift it the more easily. If you do, you will only succeed in hitting it with the edge, and the effect will be most unwelcome. Sole your club squarely on the ground and the force of impact will do the rest, granted that the ball is struck in the manner already recommended.

Approach at Fifty Yards

I. At the Top of the Swing

II. Follow Through

III. The Finish

Longer Approaches

When you have learned to play a thirty or forty yard approach with fair accuracy, you may begin to move farther away from the hole; but do not lengthen your swing more than is absolutely necessary. When you have once begun to hit the ball clean with the arm stroke, you will be astonished to find how far the ball will travel with a very small expenditure of force. Circumstances of wind and weather will naturally be taken into consideration; but generally speaking, when you find yourself between seventy and eighty yards from the hole you will have to alter your grip. Instead of holding the club in the fingers of both hands, you will have to go back to the original method employed in driving.

But this will in no way change the stroke itself. The only difference between playing a forty yard stroke and one of eighty yards, is that the swing is rather longer in the latter case. One other point may be observed as the approach grows longer. So far no mention has been made of the weight of the body, because in the shorter strokes the body is hardly employed at all. Gradually, however, as greater distance has to be covered, the weight of the body begins to be called into use.

There is very little difference in the length of the swing, and the position of the feet is only slightly modified, the left foot coming forward a little, and the right moving back. But as greater force is required, the body has to be employed; that is to say, the weight is thrown first on the right leg as club goes back, and then on the left as it comes forward. This is the whole secret of obtaining distance with the half shot, and since precisely the same means are employed in driving, the young player ought not by this time to find the difficulty insuperable.

Of course it sounds easy enough until an experiment is made, and then the weight of the body is found to be very unmanageable. Either there is a tendency to sway the whole frame backward and forward, which is entirely wrong, because it makes accuracy impossible, or else the weight of the body is thrown into the forward stroke too soon, with the result that the club comes down behind the ball, with much detriment to the turf.

You must change your center of gravity from right to left in exact accordance with the forward movement of the club, so that there is no sledge hammering or jerkiness in the stroke. And this is the most difficult part of the whole matter. In fact, you cannot attain the proper rhythmical movement if you are conscious that you are throwing your whole weight at the ball.

There is only one thing to be done, and that is to think more of the finish of the stroke than anything else. Remember that hands, arms, shoulders and everything except the toes of your right foot must be sent after the ball and continue to point in the direction of the hole long after the ball has left the club. If you really succeed in doing this, the weight of the body is naturally moved from right to left without your foreknowledge.

Approach at One Hundred Yards

I. Position

II. At the Top of the Swing

III. Coming Down

IV. Coming Down

V. Follow Through

VI. The Finish

I. Position

II. At the Top of the Swing

III. Coming Down

IV. Coming Down

V. Follow Through

VI. The Finish

The Three Quarters Shot

This half stroke will take you back to a hundred yards from the hole with ease, and then you will find yourself in a dilemma. A full shot will take you too far, and a half shot will hardly reach the green. The books advise you to play what is called the three quarters shot. As everyone who plays golf at all knows, this is quite the most dangerous stroke in the game. It is, in fact, the stroke which most beginners use for every kind of approach that is to say; they take a full swing and spare their strength.

There is, however, one way of getting out of the difficulty. At a distance of a hundred and twenty yards, let us say, you find that a full shot with your light iron will go rather too far, and the half shot which you have been practicing will not go far enough. You still may have recourse to your driving iron, which with the same half shot will send the ball the whole distance required, because it is straighter in the face, and therefore causes the ball to run farther after alighting. But then another obstacle may arise: there may be a bunker in front of the whole, so that it is impossible to play a running shot. In that case play a three quarters shot with your light iron. But don't forget that even so, the follow through is the most important part of the stroke.

The reason that the three quarters shot is so often a failure is simply this: The player begins by taking a full shot, and tries to shorten the distance by checking his swing at the moment of impact. In other words, he does not carry his club through to the finish. No stroke of that kind can ever be used with safety, although it may occasionally "come off," more by luck than good guidance. Again, some of the books regard as the distinguishing feature of the three quarters shot that the arms and shoulders are used as in the drive, but the weight of the body is not called into play. Now, this I conceive to be entirely misleading. I have already pointed out that except in the very short approaches the transference of the center of gravity from right to left is as important as in driving. And no full shot can be played with safety, simply by using the arms alone. In attempting the three quarters shot you should stand very much as you do in driving, except that the right foot may be rather more advanced, and the ball may be moved a very little farther back. The club should then be swung back, as in driving, except that the hands should not rise above the line of the shoulder; and since the object is to loft the ball, the arc described by the head of the club should be part of a smaller circle than that described by the head of the club in playing the half shot; or, to put it more simply, the head in going back should not travel so close to the ground.

Then it may be well to pause for the fraction of a second at the top of the swing in order to avoid undue haste, to which one is particularly liable in this shot. Finally, let the follow through be as complete as ever, except that the hands and club should not travel on quite so low a line as in playing the half shot. In other words, the arc described by the club after the ball is struck should correspond to the arc described in the backward swing.

The Three Quarters Shot

I. Position

II. at the Top of the Swing

III. Follow Through

IV. Follow Through

V. The Finish

I. Position

II. at the Top of the Swing

III. Follow Through

IV. Follow Through

V. The Finish

The Refinements of Iron Play

If the young player has learned to play the half stroke in the manner described, and has also mastered the three quarters shot so that he is fairly certain of the results, he will still find that there are difficulties to be overcome. But he need not trouble himself very much about them until he has acquired accuracy in the straightforward part of the short game. Not until then should he endeavor to play the high or lofting stroke or struggle with the vagaries of back spin. Still, every golfer ought to be fully equipped in every point, and he ought to know how to deal with various courses requiring various styles of play.

Back Spin and the Cut Stroke

I have hardly seen a course in America where back spin is a positive necessity. On the straightforward courses like that of the Chicago Golf Club it is possible to approach almost every hole with an ordinary light iron, because the greens are large enough and the bunkers at a sufficient distance from the hole to permit a considerable run after the ball has landed. There are other courses where the greens are small and abnormally keen, in which case no sleight of hand will enable a player to pitch his ball on to the green and keep it there.

In time, however, seaside courses will be laid out in this country, similar to the great links in England and Scotland, where the greens though large are excessively keen compared to most of our inland putting greens, and where the hole is protected by bunkers in such a way that it is absolutely necessary to play many of the approach shots with a spin in order to stop the ball on the putting green. Needless to say, in golf, as in almost every other game, no cut should be administered to the ball unless it is unavoidable.

One's object, generally speaking, is to make the ball travel as far as possible, and not to check its movements; moreover, a ball that is struck clean without any cut will roll more truly after landing than a ball which is played with a spin or from a very lofted club. Nevertheless, the cut stroke in golf is just as much part of the game as it is in billiards, and for that reason it is a pity that it is not oftener called into play by the courses which at present exist in America. In fact, it is really the mastery of this stroke which creates the distinction between the really first class golfer and the average scratch man.

Fortunately it is not hard to explain the manner of playing the shot, although it is exceedingly difficult to acquire any degree of certainty in playing it. In the ordinary approach shot the player is recommended to keep the head of the club traveling in the line of the ball's flight, both in the backward and the forward swing. He is also advised to draw the club back as near the ground as possible.

In playing the cut stroke he must neglect both these commandments. The club must be drawn across the intended line of flight, starting away from the body and coming toward it, as the ball is hit; moreover, the hands must be raised in going back and after the ball is struck, so that the swing is more vertical than horizontal, to use an unmathematical, but easily comprehensible, expression.

Strike the ball, if possible, nearer the heel than the center of the club, and aim slightly to the left of the hole. Also, in addressing the ball, face the hole more squarely even than in the ordinary short approach. Go out and practice this stroke, and, after half an hour, you will probably despair of ever being able to play it successfully. There is nothing that I can do for you except to tell you to go on practicing. There is no hidden mystery in the matter, and no easy method of acquiring the habit. If you cannot become fairly proficient in the shot, you are not skillful enough to reach the summit of ambition, and that is an end of it. Moreover, if you are unable to play the stroke with a very reasonable degree of certainty, you had better discard it altogether and use some other means of staying near the hole when the green is very fast. You may either use a very lofted club - but that, too, is uncertain - or you may harden your heart and play simply to keep out of difficulties by using the ordinary method of approach and allowing your ball to run past the hole.

If there is a bunker on the other side as well, you are indeed in a hard position; but, generally speaking, there is some means of safety if sufficient ingenuity is brought to bear on the situation.

The Cut Stroke

I. At the Top of the Swing

II. at the Top of the Swing, Front View

III. The Finish

I. At the Top of the Swing

II. at the Top of the Swing, Front View

III. The Finish

Running Up

There is another kind of approach which is used with great effect on greens like St. Andrews in Scotland, and that is the running up shot played either with the cleek or the wooden putter. This method of approaching the hole is never of much service on inland courses, where the grass is not of a fine enough nature to allow the ball to travel smoothly over it for any distance. But on seaside courses it is an invaluable part of the golfer's equipment, for it enables him very often to keep his ball near the hole when the keenness of the greens would make a lofted shot very dangerous; it is also particularly useful on windy days when it is risky to let your ball rise into the air. Here, again, the stroke is very simple, although hard to acquire.

Nothing but practice will give you the faculty of judging the strength, and that is the all-important part. For the rest, it is merely necessary to hit the ball clean, allowing, of course, for any slope in the ground, but remembering that a ball which is struck true with a wooden putter will keep its line marvelously well over any little roughness or undulation.

That is why it is often advisable to use the wooden putter, or the Musselburgh iron, as it used to be called rather contemptuously, at any distance up to forty yards or so from the hole, where there are a number of small hillocks intervening which are sure to turn a lofted shot off the line, but hardly affect a truly hit put. The wooden putter is more effective for this stroke than a cleek, because it is less likely to put any spin on the ball. But a cleek may be used in the same way where the lie does not warrant the use of the wooden club.

The Full Iron Shot

So far I have not mentioned the full shot with the iron or cleek, because, properly speaking, that comes under the head of driving. The only thing to remember in using the iron club in distinction from the ordinary driver is that a rather shorter swing is advisable. A cleek or iron is naturally a clumsier weapon than the driver, and therefore the tendency to press or to lengthen the swing is more likely to have a disastrous effect. Do not forget, then, that over swinging is particularly dangerous with an iron club, and pay special attention to the finish of the stroke.

One other point is worth mentioning: It is constantly observed that the best players are apt to take a good deal of turf with their iron shots, and the beginner generally desires an explanation of this seeming misdemeanor. Of course, when the ball is lying in a hard cup it is impossible not to take a certain amount of the grass with the ball. But even with a good lie you may often see an expert cut up a regular blanket of turf.

First of all, then, do not try to imitate him until you understand why and how it is done. If you watch him closely you will see that the turf is cut after the ball is struck, and not before; and if you ask him to explain it he will tell you, probably, that he was not conscious before the shot of any intention in the matter.

The reason is that in playing many long approaches it is necessary to land on the green without running very far, and in order to achieve the combination it is necessary to play a chop stroke; not, be it understood, the kind of stroke described above as the cut shot, for there the club is drawn across the line of flight, and the stroke is only advisable in playing with a half swing. Here the club is swung in the ordinary way, as in driving, except that the motion is rather more vertical than usual, and the follow through is checked by contact with the ground. The advantages of the stroke are twofold: In the first place, you can check the roll on the ball to a certain extent without playing across the line of flight, which is particularly difficult when a full swing is employed, and at the same time the direction is more certain; secondly, you not only do not spoil the carrying power of the stroke, but you actually impart an extra strength by the force of impact with the ground, and so you succeed in playing a shot which is often exceedingly useful; that is, one with a long straight carry and a short roll.

Do not, however, attempt this stroke in soft ground, and do not consciously attempt to cut the turf, for in that case you will probably do it before you hit the ball, with quite the wrong result.

Summary

To sum up, then: In learning to approach select an ordinary light iron, and use that alone. Begin with short approaches and a very short swing, and gradually lengthen the stroke as it becomes necessary to cover more distance. Do not attempt a three quarters shot until you are proficient in your half strokes.

Always remember that the shorter the swing the greater the accuracy; and the more uniform the style of your clubs, the less room is there for error.

Be particularly careful not to force, and never take your eye off the ball until the stroke is finished, for the shorter the stroke the more apt are you to look at the hole instead of the ball.

Above all, finish your stroke out to the end. The follow through is of supreme importance in approaching. When you have learned to play the straightforward approach - and not until then - you may begin to practice the cut stroke, the high lofting stroke and the running up game.

CHAPTER IV
PUTTING

The putt is used for putting the ball in the hole or closer to the hole from the green or the fringe of the green. The golfer adjusts his putt to fit the circumstances of the play such as distance to the hole and slope of the green. The face of the club starts *square to the target line. The club goes straight* back and straight through along the same path like a pendulum. Every sort of instrument, from a respectable wooden putter to a croquet mallet or a billiard cue, has been used, and used successfully, on the putting green. No style or position is left untried; no muscle unturned which may help the ball to its much coveted resting place. Some grip the shaft at the top, some at the bottom; some stand severely erect in the attitude of command, some crouch low over the recalcitrant *gutta percha*, that they may the better coax or control its movements. One eminent player uses his cleek as if it were an eggspoon; another astonishes his partner in a foursome by putting in a negligence fashion with one hand.

Every way is right which fulfills the purpose in view, and each individual is convinced that his style is the best. It is rather rash, then, to offer advice upon a subject which admits of so much diversity of opinion. The novice will listen to the expert when he lectures upon driving or approaching, for there his superiority grants him a privilege to preach. But when it comes to putting, the part of the game which to the outsider is not only very dull, but absurdly easy, and when the preacher misses in practice an eighteen inch put which any child could kick into the hole, the beginner is very apt to reserve his judgment and cleave to his own self cultivated style.

Still, even in putting there is a right and a wrong way. Take the test of experience, and you will find that in the long run the man who puts in the approved method wins the day. The man who handles his putter as he would a spade may do wonders on ordinary occasions when nothing depends upon the result; he is hopeless as soon as the strain begins to tell.

Position

Begin, then, by standing just as you have been instructed to do in playing a short wrist shot; that is, with the line of your feet at an angle of 45° with the line of the hole. Place the ball a little in front of your right foot; in fact, the feet being closer than in driving, the ball should be almost as near one as the other.

The Hands

The hands should grasp the shaft just as they do in the short approach; the club should be held in the fingers of each hand, and the hands should be as close together as possible. Some of the best players, both in putting and approaching, allow the right to overlap the left, in order to have but one fulcrum. This method is not recommended to the average player, because it requires a delicacy and firmness combined, which only comes with long practice. Be careful not to grip the club too loosely, nor to allow the thumbs or forefingers to stray down the shaft. In putting, as in driving, there comes a time when you are totally unconscious of any grip on the club at all; the driver or putter becomes part of the player, just as a good rider seems to be one with his horse. For the ordinary mortal, however, the club is something extraneous and apart, and the method of grasping it is a matter of considerable importance.

The most common fault in putting comes from slackness. Whenever your ball does not travel straight from the club, and especially when you find yourself varying greatly in strength, look to your hands you are probably holding too loosely, so that the head of the club turns ever so slightly as the ball is struck, which accounts for vagaries in strength and direction. Of course you must not hold your club as in a vise, nor must you allow either hand to dominate the other. The grip should be even with both hands just tight enough to obviate any turning of the head, and not so tight as to stop the circulation or freeze the muscles. The position of the feet and hands should not be varied with the club, but in other respects there are a few differences in attitude, according to the kind of putter you employ.

The Choice of Club

You may put with a cleek, a putting cleek, an iron putter or a wooden putter. By a cleek I mean any weapon of the driving iron tribe which you may happen to fancy. It may be a straight-faced driving iron, a driving mashie or a common cleek. What differentiates it from a putting cleek is that it has the ordinary driving shaft, and the angle of the head and the shaft is more obtuse. The putter of every description is an upright club, requiring rather a different attitude of body. It may sound rather an absurd statement, but general practice, I believe, will bear me out, when I maintain that if you are going to use the iron club at all for putting, the ordinary driving cleek is a better weapon than the iron putter, which is made especially for the purpose.

The Advantage of the Cleek

In the first place, the iron putter, pure and simple, is useless on greens that are at all rough and heavy, because it keeps the ball closer to the ground than any other club. Secondly, the face is so smooth and straight that, unless the stroke is very accurate, the ball is apt to glide from it to right or left. Thirdly, both the head and the shaft are dead; they give no life to the ball, as the wooden putter does. You will observe that these objections would have no weight if you were playing on a billiard table; but putting greens are not billiard tables. Even the best of them have their rough or grassy spots, and therefore the club that does not keep the ball too close to the ground is preferable. Also, if you are to use an iron club at all, there should be that driving power which, in the wooden putter, is supplied by the material from which the head is made.

But there is yet another reason for the use of the ordinary cleek, which I have never seen advanced in any book on the subject. In the second chapter I recommended a certain uniformity of weight and lie for all the wooden driving clubs. For a similar reason I believe that the more your putter resembles your light iron in weight and lie, the more regular will be your short game.

The Stroke

In putting you should begin, as in approaching, about thirty yards from the hole, and work in the opposite direction. Saving the fact that in one case you are playing with a cleek, and in the other with an iron, the stroke should be almost identical. The club should be drawn back close to the ground and in a straight line; the backward movement it can hardly be called a swing any longer should be deliberate, but not too long. Most beginners are inclined to draw the club too far back, both in putting and approaching. The left wrist should bend very little, but both the right wrist and elbow should be brought into use. In following the stroke through, the hands should be brought well forward, and the head of the club should point toward the hole.

Practice this stroke from the extreme edge of the putting green, and then as you come nearer the hole you will find that there is only a difference of degree between playing an approach of seventy yards and negotiating a put of seven feet. It is hardly necessary to add that the eye must be kept fixed upon the ball, especially as you get nearer the hole. When you have a bad attack of inaccuracy in your short puts, as every golfer has from time to time, you will generally find that you are looking at the hole instead of the ball.

FINISH OF THE APPROACH PUT

The mistake is peculiarly apt to happen in playing your short puts, because the hole is so close that it catches your eye unawares. Look hard at your ball, then, and make up your mind to hit it clean. If you succeed you will very seldom miss the hole at short range.

Only one thing more: In putting with a cleek it is advisable to strike the ball rather toward the heel of the club, because the balance is in that direction. With a wooden putter strike rather nearer the toe than the heel.

If you use your cleek for putting in the manner suggested, you will observe that there is nothing of the pendulum motion which is often recommended in the books. The club does not swing evenly backward and forward in front of the body, but is pushed, as it were, away from the body toward the hole. This style of putting is really more like the forward stroke in cricket than anything else; and just as in cricket you keep the left arm and shoulder forward to avoid a pull, so in putting you should, if anything, bend your left elbow a little in dachshund fashion, and thus keep the left shoulder well over the ball. And whatever else you do, do not rest the right elbow on the hip. Your arms should work perfectly freely from the shoulders, and the body should in no way enter into the stroke; if you allow yourself to come forward at all except with your arms, in striking the ball, the results will be most disastrous. And since it is obvious that the body must move if the elbow is resting on the hip, you must discard that method of play at all risks. I cannot conceive where it first originated.

There is hardly a single good putter among all the first class players in Great Britain who does not keep his arms entirely free; and yet I have seen numberless beginners in this country who have been told to put in that way by their professional advisers.

The Iron Putter

In using a putting cleek or an iron putter or a wooden putter, it is necessary to stand more erect because the club itself is more upright; therefore you must be closer to your ball, and your feet should be less far apart.

The best way of using any of these three weapons is rather different from the method recommended above. Your regular putter is a different club entirely from an iron or a cleek, and so you have to learn what a new stroke is practically.

POSITION FOR THE IRON PUTTER

121

AFTER THE STROKE

The Pendulum Stroke

The best putters who use the Pendulum iron club employ the wrists to a considerable extent, and let the head swing backward and forward like a pendulum. There is no doubt that this is a very effective method, especially on very true greens. The only objection that can be raised against it is that it requires great delicacy of touch.

The club is not pushed after the ball, as in the first case, but is swung by the action of the wrists; and you will find that the smallest predominance in the strength of the grip with either hand will cause the ball to reflect from its proper line. In order to preserve accuracy the shaft must be held equally firmly in either hand, and neither arm must be brought too much into the stroke.

There is, it seems to me, another objection on general principles to the use of the iron putter, and that is the difference already shown between the short approach and the put. You cannot blend the two as you would if you used a cleek to put with.

The best iron putter is probably the Park patent with the bent neck. It enables you to hit the ball rather more squarely, and does away in great measure with the tendency to let the ball glide off the surface.

The Wooden Putter

But of all the putters, there is not one which is as trustworthy as the oldest of all - the wooden putter.New clubs for use on the green are invented from time to time, and win adherents, but in the long run the wooden putter holds its own. And this is the reason: If you are going to use a short, heavy, upright club at all, it is better to use one that gives a certain life to the ball. This is particularly essential in playing long approach puts, where the elasticity of the wooden face keeps the ball running over any casual roughness which may come in the way.

Moreover, unless your greens are very true, the wooden club has a great advantage in that it does not keep the ball quite so close to the ground as the iron putter. A great many players find it advisable to use an iron club for short puts, even when they employ the wood everywhere else. That is simply a question of taste. Confidence is the main requisite for steadiness in holing short puts, and if you are not certain of one club, it is better to take another that you imagine you can rely upon.

The position and method for the use of the wooden putter are practically the same as in the case of the iron putter or putting cleek. Do not forget, however, to hit the ball slightly toward the toe of the club, or at all events, avoid striking it with the heel.

POSITION FOR THE WOODEN PUTTER

The Distinction between Courses

Great latitude, as may be observed, Is permissible in the choice of clubs for use on the putting green. There is this much to be said, however: On courses in Scotland and England it would be perfectly safe to recommend the wooden putter in preference to all others, since the best links are all by the sea. In America, so many of the courses are inland, or rather, so few are near the sea, that a strong distinction has to be drawn between seaside and inland putting greens. Unless the soil is of a sandy nature, it is wrong to begin life with a wooden putter. After a great many years it may be possible to get the same fine grass inland as is found on seaside courses; but even that is very doubtful. For the present at least, the coarser and stubblier nature of the best lawn grass debars the effective use of the wooden putter. And yet you will find it very difficult to play your long puts with the ordinary iron putter, especially if the greens are at all heavy. The ball stays too near the ground, and its strength is affected by any unevenness, and especially by long grass.

The best club for inland greens is therefore the genuine cleek with a driving shaft, cut short if necessary for convenience sake; it enables you to get the necessary distance without any great exertion, and it also allows the ball to travel more evenly over strong grass.

It must be remembered, of course, that in recommending any particular club for putting purposes, nothing more is intended than an expression of opinion. I know numbers of excellent players who disagree with me and who support their judgment by an irritating display of accuracy on the green. Still, since beginners have no prejudice in favor of one club or the other, it is just as well that they should choose that one whose use has been sanctioned by the majority. Now, on sandy soil the wooden putter probably has the preference among first class players, and the cleek or some similar iron weapon is a good second. The regular iron putter, with its straight face and upright shaft, is not patronized to any great extent by the faculty. If you are going to use an iron putter at all, it is better to get what is known as a putting cleek, a sort of cross between a driving cleek and an iron putter, or else one of Park's patent clubs, with the crooked neck.

The Line of the Put

And finally, remember to look at the ball.
Too much care over the line of your put is a
dangerous thing. Make up your mind as to your
direction first, and then when you address the ball,
look once at the hole and once at some intervening
point of the line which you have chosen, and then
devote yourself entirely to hitting the ball clean.
Many players examine their puts from both ends.
But I hardly think that this is a good plan unless you
cannot decide easily upon the line by looking at it
behind the ball. In ordinary cases it is only
confusing to examine it from both points of view.
Be very careful to place the head of your club
evenly on the ground, and hit your ball with
confidence, and you will be surprised to find how
many times it will find the hole.

Summary

To sum up, then: Choose the club that suits you best, but do not use a wooden putter on inland greens unless they are in perfect condition. Do not rest your right elbow on your hip. In using a regular putter stand erect and swing the club more or less like a pendulum; in using a cleek, or any driving club, get rather more over the ball with the shoulders and push the arms toward the hole.

Do not put entirely with the wrists. The arms and even the shoulders should enter into the stroke. Do not study the line of your put too long. Think more of hitting your ball cleans than of anything else. Keep your eye on the ball.

Photographed by R. W. Hawks, Edinburgh

MR. JOHN BALL, PUTTING

CHAPTER V
MISCELLANEOUS SUGGESTIONS

It is always hard for the experienced player in any game to sympathize with the difficulties of the beginner. In golf, the only way in which the expert can in any way put himself in the duffer's place is by playing a few holes with a set of clubs such as is usually sold to the unsuspicious novice. He will then come to the conclusion that there is nothing extraordinary in the in ability of the struggling beginner to achieve the desired result; on the contrary, it is surprising that with such implements he succeeds in doing anything even passably well. Golf clubs are turned out by the million in these days, and anything short of a broomstick is considered well enough for the young player to go out and break.

The Selection of Clubs

There is a certain hindrance of in the way of the novice, from the very nature of things. He would probably use up a larger number of the fine shafts and delicately turned heads that are made for men who know the difference between a good club and a bad one. And so he is generally persuaded by his friends to select a badly shaped lump of wood, miscalled a driver, thinking that one weapon is as good as another for his purpose, so long as the chances of breakage are as far as possible eliminated. And yet it is quite a mistaken idea to suppose that every beginner must sow his wild oats to the extent that is usually taken for granted. If he goes out determined to drive the ball at least a quarter of a mile at first sight, and is content with nothing short of a full set of contortions in imitation of what he imagines to be a St. Andrews swing and after all, that is the course that most beginners do pursue then his only chance of reducing his account with the club maker to reasonable proportions, is to choose what Virgil would call no small part of a tree, and do his best with it. In this way he may avoid great pecuniary loss, but his best will be exceedingly bad. If, on the other hand, he has read the first chapter of this book and has inwardly digested it, he will begin quietly with a half swing, and will so restrain his force that it will be quite unnecessary to break any clubs at all.

Indeed, if the beginner really takes the advice there offered to him there is no reason in the world why he should not be far less destructive to his clubs than the good player who hits cleaner, but with far greater force.

Accordingly, if you really mean to play the game for what it is worth, do not be content with whatever your club maker may offer you. The ordinary price of a driver in Scotland is five shillings and sixpence, in this country between a dollar and a half and two dollars. But it may be taken for granted that at least seventy five percent of the clubs which are sold at that price are quite unfit to play with.

The driver which you have made to order for double the price is generally worth a whole stack full of the readymade article. If possible, then, the beginner should either procure a club from some more experienced friend, and have it copied, or he should insist upon the club maker supplying him with a club of reasonable proportions.

The Weight

In order to choose most wisely, think first of all about the weight. It would not be an exaggeration to say that two thirds of the men who are attempting to play golf in America at the present time are using clubs which are far too heavy for the purpose. I constantly hear it said when any remonstrance is offered: "With my style I need a heavy club," or, "I am too weak to use a light club," or, "With my strength I really ought to be able to play with a heavy driver," and so on in a similar strain. If you really do find that you can do better with a heavily weighted club, you should at once change your style of play; there must be something radically wrong with it. For there is a universal consensus of opinion among good players upon the subject. Some, of course, use heavier clubs than others; it stands to reason that a man with very powerful arms and wrists can swing a club which a weaker player could not use at all. But even allowing for differences in individual strength, a careful examination of the drivers of all the good players in the world would show a surprisingly small variety in weight.

There is an easily understood reason why the beginner is naturally inclined to select a heavy club. He has not yet learned to sweep the ball away instead of hitting it as he would with a sledge hammer; and obviously if the ball is struck at as if it were a resisting object the heavier the club is the better will be the result. But this is not golf. It is possible, of course, to hit an occasional long ball with the sledge hammer stroke, but length must be sacrificed to accuracy, and the player who adopts this method generally goes from bad to worse, until he ruins his chances of ever becoming even a fairly good performer. The best players are also addicted at times to this hitting or chopping tendency, very often for the simple reason that they have unconsciously been using heavier clubs than they are accustomed to. Whenever this is the case it is not at all a bad plan to extract a little lead. But with the beginner or the young player who is not yet certain of his style, a more radical change is generally necessary. If he finds that he cannot get the necessary distance out of a driver of medium weight, it is almost certain that he is not sweeping the ball away at all; he is checking his swing as the club comes down instead of letting it follow through. In such a case there is nothing for him to do but to go back to first principles.

Having stated the reasons for using a light club, it is necessary to say exactly what the term implies. Advice of this sort is seldom of much service unless it is accompanied by figures. And yet the actual weight of a driver varies so much according to the balance and lie, that it is almost dangerous to be too definite. Still, a general estimate may be of some assistance. The weight of a driver head should not exceed seven ounces; the shaft should be no heavier; add the two and you will get a fairly good idea of what the whole club should weigh when a fraction of an ounce has been added for the glue and string used in splicing the two together.

I am perfectly certain that if beginners would observe these limits very carefully, they would not only get better results, but they would not risk their entire future prospects by ruining their styles at the outset. One cannot insist too strongly upon this point because, for the reasons already given, it is exceedingly hard to impress upon the young player the danger of using a heavy club.

Even the more experienced golfer is apt to forget the difference that a fraction of an ounce will make in a long match of thirty six holes. Just as in carrying a gun, an ounce or two is a matter of no importance when the morning is young, but the difference tells enormously at the end of a long day; so with a driver that is a shade too heavy, the first eighteen tee shots may be struck perfectly clean, but the last nine in the afternoon are apt to be very erratic.

And especially if a player does not possess great strength of wrist, should he be warned against the mistaken idea that extra weight in the club will make up for lack of muscle behind it. If the strong man should use a light club it is far more necessary that the weaker player should avoid a superabundance of lead. The main object is to hit the ball clean, and the distance will take care of itself. No one can be sure of a clean, steady stroke if he is using a club which is too heavy for him.

The Shaft

First, then, make up your mind as to the weight of your wooden club; and then look at the shaft; It is the fashion from time to time to adopt a thick, stiff shaft, but no one has ever explained why that should be preferable. The shaft should be as thin as possible without becoming too supple. There is a danger too of a very thin shaft losing its shape quickly, although that is not an important consideration, because it depends far more upon the quality of the wood. A good piece of split hickory ought to taper down where it joins the head without becoming supple at all. There should be a certain amount of spring, but do not select a club with the spring high up in the shaft. In trying it you ought not to feel any suppleness at all in the grip. In other words, the spring should begin about half way between the leather and the head. Very few shafts answer to this description, because so much unseasoned wood is used in the manufacture of golf clubs that it is safer to leave the shaft in a more or less clumsy form to avoid bending or breakage.

Nevertheless, even the beginner should get as good a club as possible, and if he can find a thin shaft which is not at the same time flabby, he may be fairly certain that he has got a good piece of wood. The shafts of all clubs, it may be remarked, should be made from split hickory. Various other woods have been substituted, but they have nearly always been found wanting.

Hickory combines lightness and spring with strength and durability in a way that no other wood can equal. Seeing that hickory is one of the commonest woods in America, there should be no difficulty in securing good shafts in this country. In selecting the head of a driver, the most important thing, next to the weight, is the angle which it makes with the shaft.

Here again, individual taste must be considered; but, as a general rule, the angle is far too obtuse. The result is that the player cannot stand erect and still keep the sole of the club level upon the ground. Remember that your steadiness in driving is greatly increased by standing fairly erect and using what is called an upright club; that is to say, one with not too obtuse an angle between the shaft and the head.

The Shape of the Head

As for the shape of the head, you should use a bulger with plenty of wood in it. There is a tendency among bad club makers to turn out drivers with a great deal of material in the neck, but too narrow a surface in the face. Just as the shaft should taper toward the bottom, so the part of the head which joins the shaft should be made as fine as possible, in order to impart the requisite spring.

For the purposes of the beginner, it is all important to secure a good driver, because he ought to content himself, for a time at least, with practice in driving. And at all stages of the game there is nothing which adds so much to the pleasure of the game, as the possession of a club which gives the player every chance of success in striking from the tee. But a careful selection of the other clubs in the set is really just as important, as soon as the elementary part of the game has been mastered.

The Brassey

I have already pointed out that the brassey should resemble the driver, both in weight and lie. The more uniform you can make your clubs in that respect, the greater will be your steadiness. And for that reason I would again suggest that you should discard the brassey wherever the character of the turf warrants it, and use instead either a second driver for playing through the green or the old fashioned spoon which has almost gone out of use. A spoon is simply a driver with the face a little laidback in order to raise the ball more easily, and with the shaft a trifle shorter and stiffer. Whether you employ a brassey or a spoon, it is best not to lay the face back too much, because any artificial aid in raising the ball from the ground is rather to be deprecated.

The natural movement of the swing should answer the purpose unless the ball is lying in a hole or on the downward slope of a hill. As for the superiority of the driver or spoon over the brassey, there can be little doubt that the brass on the bottom of the club must alter the distribution of the weight, and so destroy the uniformity of your wooden clubs without any compensating advantage, except in cases where the ground is so hard and rough as to injure the sole of the wooden club.

Iron Clubs

In the selection of iron clubs there is great scope for variety of taste. I have already warned the beginner against the use of a very lofted club, for reasons just stated with reference to the spoon. If you play the stroke properly, you should not require much assistance from the club itself in order to loft the ball over any ordinary obstacle. And so your approaching club should be the light iron, which you may employ for any distance, from a hundred and twenty yards down to thirty or forty. In addition to that you will need a cleek or a driving mashie for distances of about one hundred and fifty yards, and a driving iron is useful in negotiating distances which are rather shorter, and yet too long for the light iron, and also for playing all kinds of approach shots in a high wind.

The preference among good players seems at present to be in favor of the driving mashie as against the cleek, partly because the face is shorter, and therefore more accommodating when the ball is lying badly, and partly because the extra breadth of the blade admits more latitude for error. The best driving mashies are probably those which are made by Forgan and Auchterlonie, in St. Andrews. They are made without the bulge in the back, which is rather a hindrance than anything else. In fact, it is just as well to avoid all iron clubs with the bulge. They do not drive any farther, and the weight is so much concentrated that the slightest deviation from the center of the club involves a very bad stroke.

In choosing between a mashie and what is generally called a lofter, it is much better to take the former. A good mashie should weigh about as much as your light iron, and should not be excessively laid back. A lofter is made after the fashion of a soup ladle, and cannot possibly be used with great accuracy. The beginner clings to it because he finds that he can overcome obstructions with it, forgetting that with a little practice he can obtain the same results by using a less lofted mashie, where the occasion demands it, and as a general rule the ordinary light iron, which is not such a spectacular club, but infinitely more trustworthy.

Up to the present time there seems to be little sign of any great improvement on the part of American club makers upon the implements that come from Scotland, and for that reason the beginner cannot do better than look for the name of one of the great Scotch club makers. Irons are not like drivers. As far as the shape of the head goes, there is no reason why they should not be turned out by the thousand.

The name of a club maker on the head of a driver means nothing at all, because only one out of ten wooden clubs is made of properly seasoned wood, and only one out of twenty is worth the price that is paid for it. But when once a club maker has secured a good pattern for an iron club, he should be able to duplicate it forever.

Forgan, Morris and Auchterlonie, to mention only three, can always be trusted in that respect, and Simpson, at Carnoustie, turns out some excellent light irons. Forgan's driving mashie is perhaps the prettiest and most useful club of the kind that is made, and all Auchterlonie's irons are good. As for wooden clubs, it is best to buy them on the spot if you have a good club maker. The Scotch professionals control the market in that respect, because it is almost impossible for anyone to make wooden clubs who does not understand their use. The wholesale manufacture of wooden clubs may meet the enormous demand which comes from all parts of the country, as far as quantity goes, but the quality is distinctly lacking. If you have not a good professional club maker close at hand, you must do what you can with the readymade article; but there is no reason why any golf club should not secure the services of a really good professional maker.

The Choice of balls

The selection of balls is a more uncertain matter. The difficulty is two fold. The professional club makers who make a limited number of balls out of good material cannot furnish supplies to the general market; on the other hand, the firms which manufacture balls by the thousand are sure to become careless. At the present time there is no ball in this country which for all round purposes surpasses that which is made by the Silvertown Company. The material is generally good, the molding is excellent and the paint holds very well. Unfortunately one often comes across a box of Silvertowns which are not seasoned, are carelessly painted and badly pressed.

Always look carefully at the molding; if it is clean cut, the ball has probably been well pressed and will fly true. If it is shallow and indistinct, the mold has probably been worn out and the ball is not properly pressed. A good clear marking is very essential, and the paint should be applied in such a way as not to fill up the interstices. There are a number of different balls in use in America which are more or less good. The Woodley Flyer and the Black A 1 are very similar in make, but neither of them comes up to the best of the Silvertowns. Just at present there is a great demand for balls made in the Agrippa mold.

And there does seem to be some advantage in the marking, as is evidenced by the fact that balls which are remade in that mold are generally superior to any others. There is this objection, however, to the average Agrippa ball, that it does not keep either its shape or its paint as a good Silvertown.

Consequently, they make up in expense for what they gain in flying capacity. It is a good plan to lay in a store of balls so that you are certain of their being properly seasoned. But it should be remembered that it is possible to keep a ball too long. From eighteen months to two years is about the limit; after that there is a loss in weight and elasticity.

On the Playing of Matches

When you have secured a good, set of clubs and the right kind of ball, and have even learned to play a steady game, there is still much that you can do to improve upon your knowledge and enjoyment of golf. First of all, play the game for the sake of the personal encounter. For, after all, golf is a trial of skill, and not a solitary mode of exercise. For that reason, give up, as far as possible, counting your score, and devote your time to playing matches. In arranging a game you should, for your own advantage, play with your superiors, but it is both useless and discouraging to encounter a man who can give you very great odds. One stroke a hole is the limit which can be given in order to make a match interesting and even that is putting it at a high figure. A match can be keenly exciting between two men who differ by six strokes in the round, but anything above that is apt to rob the game of its interest. Still, if you are a very bad player, but can yet be relied upon to a certain extent, you may improve your game immensely by playing in foursomes with men who can give you very great odds. It is astonishing how successfully a pair, consisting of a first class and a fourth class player, can encounter two players of the second class. But whatever you do, never play a man on level terms that ought either to give you odds or receive them from you. That is a very common mistake which is constantly being made, because there are certain players who object, for some unknown reason, to taking odds in any game.

To obviate this habit, the custom of betting, as long as it is kept within well defined limits, is most beneficial. A man may be willing to take a beating on even terms when he loses nothing thereby, either in purse or in pride, and stands to win a good deal of glory should he chance to gain the victory. But if he is playing for a stake, be it ever so small, the commercial instinct is aroused, and he will take all the odds that his opponent will concede. In the latter case he may improve his game; in the former he certainly will not. The only way to become a good golfer is to play every match for all it is worth, and in order to do this you should always arrange the odds as fairly as possible.

Giving and taking odds

The practice of giving and receiving bisques is by no means a bad method of handicapping in match play because it gives the inferior player a chance of playing his opponent on even terms as long as he likes, and at the end of the game if he has won the match without the aid of his bisques he is entitled to all possible credit. The better player cannot then argue that the game had no interest for him, as he might if it were really played without odds at all. And from the expert's point of view it is by no means a bad plan; for he is forced to play the game from the very start. If he is giving his opponent half a stroke a hole, he is apt to play very carelessly in the holes where there are no strokes ; but when he is giving bisques he cannot afford to throw away a single chance, because he must not only divide these holes, but must win them if possible with a stroke to spare. But whatever the system of handicapping maybe, always take as much as you can get, and give as little as will be accepted, and you will still find that if there is anything at all at stake, you will have to play a good game to win. In that way you will soon become a good match player; otherwise you will probably improve more slowly, and in the meantime get much less, enjoyment out of the game.

The Etiquette of Golf

The etiquette of golf should also be most carefully studied. You may not be a good player, but you may at least equal the very best exponents of the game in your manner of playing it. As far as the rules go, be most scrupulous, even in an ordinary practice game, to observe the strict letter of the law, and never take any concession from your opponent. If he asks you to remit a penalty, that is another matter. You ought to be in a position; however, to refuse him everything that is not his by right. On the other hand, do not quibble about technical points which obviously do not enter into the spirit of the rule. For instance, no one, whose mind is not clouded by enthusiasm, could ever think of claiming a hole because his opponent accidentally drops a club in a bunker where his ball is lying" some distance away. Be very careful, however, to do nothing, either in action or in words, which may annoy your opponent and so spoil his game.

There are many subtle ways of irritating him if he is at all a nervous player, and to tell the truth, there are a number of prominent golfers who are not above .employing these questionable methods; not that they would intentionally put him off a stroke, but they seem to think that remarks which are quite unnecessary, and which may prove rather annoying, are perfectly legitimate. In England or Scotland players who resort to these devices are very easily dealt with.

No one plays with them. Here it is not so easy to act in that way, because there are so many tournaments and prize competitions that for at least half your season you cannot choose either your partner or your opponent. I have actually heard a player admit that he sometimes plays more slowly than is absolutely necessary, because it may assist him to defeat his adversary. If he only thought about it for a moment he would see that such a course is really just as reprehensible as a deliberate attempt to interfere with a player's swing. He ought, on the contrary, to be particularly careful avoid undue deliberation, which might unintentionally be a cause of annoyance.

The Duties of On-Lookers

It may be useful to point out here to onlookers in the game that they also have duties to perform. If they care to follow a match they are bound in all courtesy to study the wishes of the players. The most common fault which may be found is in the position which is nearly always assumed by ignorant bystanders when a player is making a stroke. They naturally stand behind the ball in the direct line of flight, which is the one place they ought to avoid. They should either stand behind the player's back where he cannot see them at all, or right in front of him, so that they do not catch his eye as he swings backward. And above all, they should not move or speak until the shot is played. There is ample time for conversation between shots without disturbing the player just as he is about to hit the ball. It would be most beneficial if a few suggestions of this nature were incorporated in the rules upon the etiquette of golf, and especially if a diagram were made showing exactly where the onlooker should stand when a stroke is being played.

CHAPTER VI
TRAINING AND TOURNAMENT PLAY

There was a time when golf was played as a recreation. In those days any one would have ridiculed a definite system of training for the big events. But now that the game has become the main business of our lives, any course of exercise or rule of diet which may bring enhanced opportunities of victory must be taken into the most serious consideration. And yet in matters of training golf is unlike any of the other great games which we pursue with short intervals for business.

No one can consume an unlimited amount of tobacco and still row in a college race with any chance of success. The captain of a football team would be foolish if he did not discourage pastry and strong drink. Even the devotees of the polo field must refrain from Pommery at every meal. With golf it is quite another matter. Some of our best players are tobacco fiends. One can hardly picture Mr. F. G. Tait without his pipe, or Mr. Hilton shorn of his cigarette. Our best scores are often made after nights of whist and Scotch whisky; indeed, there are those who believe that the true secret of success is somehow bound up with liberal ideas upon the subject of the national drink of Caledonia.

This view of the question impresses itself with startling emphasis upon athletes in this country who have been accustomed to look upon the traditions of the training table as upon the unalterable laws of the Medes and Persians. And they are apt to feel very indignant when in spite of careful diet they are defeated by less scrupulous opponents who, by all the rules of retribution, ought to be incapable of hitting the ball at all. As a general rule, training is simply a matter of habit. Most American oarsmen would be rather surprised if they could see the members of a college eight, at Oxford, supposed to be in strict training, drinking liberal potations of homebrewed ale during dinner, and washing it down with a glass or two of the richest port that the common room can supply. And I imagine that the captain of an American football or baseball team would be scandalized to hear that in the case of the 'varsity cricket elevens and football fifteens, in England, such a thing as training in any shape or form is practically unknown. Possibly, the great English universities err rather in the direction of liberality. But after all, a game ought to be played for the sake of recreation, and not studied like a profession. Moreover, I doubt very much whether the winning" capacity of any football team is greatly increased by any close restrictions in the matter of diet. One understands, of course, that smoking" should be prohibited among college eights, because the consumption of tobacco, particularly on the part of young men, is apt to injure the wind.

But in games where there is no continued strain upon the lungs, the question of smoking is totally irrelevant. However that may be, it is perfectly natural that golf, being a game of recent importation into America, has not yet become a subject for any strict laws upon the subject of training. Believing firmly, as I do, that in every sport latitude in diet and habits of life is strongly to be recommended, both because such a course is consistent with success, and because it is not reasonable to regard any game or sport in too serious a light, I have no intention of writing any prescriptions for use before tournaments. Even if such advice were desirable in dealing with rowing or foot ball, the circumstances which surround the game of golf would rob it of all its value.

The players in this case are generally men of mature years and settled habits, who could not change their methods of life without serious discomfort. Moreover, it must always be remembered that the mental condition is of far greater importance than physical fitness. You cannot play golf if you are worried in mind, and therefore my first exhortation to anyone about to enter a tournament or play an important match is that he should divest himself entirely of all thoughts bearing upon any subject except the matter immediately in hand. Concentration of purpose is quite as necessary as strength of arm. Let no one suppose, however, that a sound physical condition is not of supreme importance.

A blind man, a cripple or a habitual drunkard is not likely to win many trophies on the links. Whoever is looking for advice upon the playing of tournaments is at least a person of some athletic sense. He knows that the better his health is, the greater are his chances of success; he knows also that practice makes perfect, if he has read his copybook. These are truisms which are granted at the outset. But I desire chiefly to point out that the average man who leads an upright and sober life would act very foolishly to change any of his ordinary habits before a tournament. If he is a smoker, he should on no account discard tobacco; if he is accustomed to stimulants, he should drink just as much as, and no more than, he does on ordinary occasions. Possibly someone may confront me with the argument that both smoking and drinking are injurious to the health. If anyone thinks so he would be wise to abjure them both, but he should abjure them qua man and not qua golfer. If, on the other hand, these pleasant habits are not found to hurt the system in other departments of life, it is impossible to see why they should interfere with the game of golf. In fact, I would even go a step further and say that they are positively conducive to good play.

Take, for instance, a man who smokes a certain amount of tobacco every day; when he comes to a tournament, or to a close match, he will find a great deal of help and consolation in his pipe or his cigarette, as the case may be. Another player, perhaps, is accustomed during a hard day's golf to fortify him in various ways at luncheon or at dinner, when the game is over.

To such a person I would never say, Omit your whisky and soda during a tournament. I should be much more inclined to admonish him to take two where before he took one. The mental strain of a tournament increases the ordinary fatigue of playing at least one hundred percent, and therefore those accustomed to stimulant of any sort should increase rather than diminish the dose. As for diet, there is hardly anything which a man who is playing thirty six holes a day cannot and may not eat with safety. Good food, and plenty of it, is the watchword for every golfer. It may be necessary, however, to guard against one error, for which Mr. Horace Hutchinson, in perfect innocence, is partly responsible.

Some years ago, when first class players were not so plentiful and record breaking was not a matter of everyday occurrence, Mr. Leslie Balfour Melville, in playing for the medal of the Royal and ancient Golf Club, at St. Andrews, broke the existing record for medal play, by completing the eighteen holes in eighty five strokes. It was hardly expected that such a score could be beaten. Mr. Alexander Stuart, however, had not started when Mr. Balfour Melville's card was handed in. With excellent discretion he ordered himself a steak and a pint of champagne, which he discussed at leisure, and thereafter surprised everyone by returning a score of eighty three, breaking by two strokes the record which had been established only two hours before.

Mr. Horace Hutchinson, in compiling the Badminton book on golf, was mindful of this occurrence, and, while publishing no names, he printed a picture strongly resembling Mr. Stuart in the act of eating that fateful luncheon, and held it up as an example to all future aspirants for golfing honors. It is years now since the medal record at St. Andrews stood as high as eighty six, and so I may be forgiven for mentioning" proper names ; Mr. Hutchinson may also forgive me if I point out that his advice on that subject is good relatively, but not absolutely. It was only a chance suggestion in any case; yet that picture of the steak and the man, and above all, the familiar pint bottle, has something so comforting and attractive about it, that many readers have fastened their attention upon that piece of advice to the exclusion of everything else. In reality, it is mainly a question of climate. In the cold air of Scotland, no harm can come of seeking adventitious aid from Heidsieck's special cuvee, or even the more democratic Glenlivet. In America we are accustomed to play golf in almost tropical weather, and under such circumstances stimulants should be administered after, rather than before, the contest.

Anyone who is in the habit of playing games is aware that on a hot day, and especially after taking exercise, the smallest modicum of alcohol is apt to affect the eye, and therefore it by no means follows that what maybe done with success in Scotland can be ventured upon with impunity in America.

In hot weather it is well to be rather careful between rounds, and when an important match has to be played in the afternoon, a light luncheon is particularly advisable: In other respects, however, care in training may be greatly overdone. Even in rowing it is customary to administer champagne to a crew after a hard race; and in golf, where the strain is of far longer duration, a hard day's play may very reasonably be rewarded by such restoratives as may be found most acceptable. The regulation of practice in the game itself is more important than any restriction of diet. Golf has been taken up, like most other pursuits in America, with an enormous amount of enthusiasm; and the constant tendency is in the direction of overplay. In England and Scotland there are very few weeks in the year when golf is impracticable, and only a month or two when the temperature is either disagreeably hot or cold. Yet the best players very rarely devote more than four or five weeks in the spring and a similar time in the autumn to the real practice of the game.

During the rest of the year they may play an occasional match, but they are seldom on the links for two days in succession. In America, those who play golf at all do it for six months at a time, and they are surprised to find that they cannot keep up their form for the whole of that period.

If golf becomes a regular part of your existence, two or at most three days a week is quite enough for its exercise, if you desire to preserve either your skill or your interest. And even then it would be advisable to take an occasional week off and get away entirely from the atmosphere of the game. When it comes to tournament play you should order all your practice with a view to reaching the top of your game just at the right moment. It is fatal to strike twelve a month before the important event.

Consequently, if you find that you are actually improving too quickly, you should be all the more careful not to overdo it. Most golfers will tell you that they play the strongest and most consistent game about the end of the third week from the time that they began regular practice; so that you must pursue a course of this nature (remembering always that we are speaking now with regard to success in an important tournament, and not from the point of view of any pleasure that you may derive from the pastime). Granted that you have already developed your game to the limit of its capacity, you should give up playing altogether about two months before the tournament in question, and for four or five weeks you should, if possible, keep away entirely from the sight of a golf links ;even the discussion of the game should be avoided.

You require a complete mental and physical rest from this most arduous pursuit. You must not, however, give up every kind of physical exercise. One constantly hears that tennis and cricket and baseball spoil golf. This is an entirely mistaken idea. Of course, you cannot play cricket or baseball and golf interchangeably. If you do you will fail in both. But if you have already acquired a good golfing style, you may play any other game for a year, and then go back to golf and find that you have gained rather than lost by the diversion. The fact is that the constant practice of any single game develops only a certain set of muscles, and these muscles begin to lose their vigor when they are called too frequently into play; to speak technically, the man becomes stale. As soon as any symptom of this flabbiness becomes apparent, the golf club should be discarded for some other weapon.

Play another game, then, for four or five weeks, and then' with about a fortnight to spare come back to golf and. you will find yourself assailed by a new access of vigor and keenness. From that time on until the final contest you may play steadily and often, but it is well not to exceed thirty six holes a day, or five days a week; in fact, even that limit is rather liberal. Do not play too many matches in the meantime that you are particularly anxious to win, for that will use up a large part of your mental energy; and employ at least a third of the time in practicing, with single clubs, the strokes that you find most difficult. If you follow this advice you will probably find yourself in the best condition when the tournament begins.

But that is not all you have to consider. It is absolutely necessary that your mind should also be clear and untroubled. There is no game in the world where the mental strain is so great. It begins with the first day of the tournament, and lasts through every hole until the final stroke is played. In entering' the game, therefore, you must make up your mind to two things: First of all, you must give your opponent no possible chance through any carelessness on your part. However easy the match may seem, you must play your hardest Remember that you not only want to win, but you want to win easily, so that you use up as little of your store of energy as possible.

That is where many players lose themselves in tournaments where there are several rounds of match play. They forget that one victory only leads to another contest, and they often allow a much weaker opponent to bring the match to a close finish, thus wearing them out needlessly. In the second place, concentrate your attention upon the game itself, and never think for a moment of the final result. This is the hardest task of all, but it must be accomplished if you desire to win. As soon as you begin to think of the possibility of defeat, you will become over anxious, and you will lose your freedom of style. It may seem almost impossible for a player to divest himself entirely of all hopes and fears for the future. But it is a faculty which comes readily with practice in tournament play. Some acquire it more quickly than others.

There are several cases in the history of golf championships of victories won by very young men. Mr.P. C. Anderson and Mr. Allen were both of tender golfing years when they defeated all the other amateurs of Great Britain. It is seldom, however, that the necessary confidence and concentration come to a man until he has had several years of experience in big" matches and that is why there are probably more first class players over the age of thirty than there are below it. There are other habits which even the youngest player may possess, with the exercise of a little intelligence. There is a strong tendency among American players of the first rank in the direction of extreme caution and deliberation in tournament play. It requires no argument to prove that slowness is for every reason a thing to be discouraged for the sake of the general welfare. But apart from the good of your fellow creatures, you have your own chances of success to consider, and you are assuredly waging war upon yourself if you get beyond a certain point in exercising care.

The fault arises not from your caution in match play, but more probably from a want of speed and freedom in ordinary practice. There is nothing which retards a man's improvement in the game so much as a lack of freedom. It is a matter of common observation that even a good golfer holes his short puts with far greater accuracy when he is not trying than when he has the strain of an important match upon him.

In the same way the indifferent player swings more freely at a daisy than at a ball. Now, if you cramp yourself by excess of care in an ordinary game, as so many young players do, how much more will you check your natural impulses in a tournament! Therefore if you have the main end in view, you will prefer to play quickly and swing freely, even to the verge of carelessness in your every day round, so that when the occasion does really call for deliberation you will be able to put a certain restraint upon yourself without entirely losing your freedom. It is an extraordinary fact that a small and inconsiderable gutta percha ball has the most paralyzing effect upon the minds and muscles of sane and healthy men, causing them to tremble and grow rigid before it. This unnatural, yet universal, obsession can only be overcome by constant practice.

You must learn to rid yourself of this terror by pretending" to disregard it. Go up to the ball and hit it just as if you were not in the least afraid of it. Assume a freedom of manner, even if it belies your feelings, and in time you will break down the influence of the bugbear to such an extent that even in an important match you will bear yourself with courage and indifference. You must be careful, on the other hand, not to overdo the quickness of your play in practice.

That is to say, you may swing freely and address your ball, especially on the putting green, with speed and decision ; but do not get too much into the habit of racing around the links, because if you do you will find the waiting which is a necessary part of tournament play, excessively irksome. Even with the best arrangements, the progress of the various couples in a large competition must be somewhat slow, and if you have not inured yourself to the tedium of long waits, such as you may suffer any day at the high hole at St. Andrews, or on any teeing ground at North Berwick, you will find yourself the victim of much inward irritation.

Of two contradictories, therefore, in spite of the logic books, you must choose both. In practice, accustom yourself to playing quickly and freely. Learn also in practice to play slowly. As a result you will be able on great occasions to add something of caution to your game, without suffering from what has been well termed ball shyness; and you will also be in a position to wait for a slow couple in front, or for the many deliberations of your opponent, without losing that equanimity which is indispensable to success.

Summary

To sum up, then, I should advise every golfer to live a healthy life. Thereafter it is unnecessary to change in any way your habits of existence with a view to success in a competition. Do not play too much, and above all, do not reach the top of your game too soon. Learn to concentrate your attention upon each stroke, and not upon the general result. Finally, practice the utmost freedom of swing and address in ordinary play, so that you may exercise deliberation in competition, without becoming abnormally slow. But do not accustom yourself so much to rapidity that the waits in a tournament affect your nerves.

CHAPTER VH
THE MAKING OF A NEW COURSE,

When the number of Scotchmen who have crossed the Atlantic is fully considered, it is rather surprising that the royal and ancient game should have been imported so recently as 1890 or thereabouts. It was really two years later that a genuine interest in golf was aroused by the organizing of clubs for the purpose of its propagation; and the United States Golf Association has only been in existence for three seasons. Once started, however, the devotion to the game became almost a craze.

At the time of writing nearly a hundred clubs have joined the association, and the number will in all probability be doubled in the course of the next twelve months. To an Englishman, who, in the last decade, has seen innumerable golf courses spring up like mushrooms over every county in Great Britain, the membership of the association may appear disappointingly small.

But when it is remembered that it is as easy, from a financial point of view, to form a hundred clubs in England as it is to place one on a firm basis in America, the strides made by the association in the short period of three years must be taken to indicate a love of the pastime which far exceeds the ordinary short lived boom so often accorded to any new fad in this country.

The Difficulties to be Overcome

The difficulties of securing a suitable course, and of maintaining it when secured, can hardly be realized by anyone who has been accustomed to find golf links readymade along the coast of Great Britain. Since most courses in America are of necessity inland, and since the very best soil can only yield the requisite quality of turf, the land which is bought by an incipient golf club, instead of being practically worthless for any other purpose, as is so often the case in Scotland, has a very high value as farming property. In the second place, the business instincts of the average American make it incumbent upon him to seek his amusement within a thirty mile radius of his down town office; and, as everyone knows, vacant lots within such a radius of any large city are ruinously expensive. And so it is no uncommon thing for a golf club to pay down $50,000 in hard cash before a ball is struck.

And that is only the beginning. You may get two hundred acres of fine old pasture, perfectly drained and full of natural hazards. You are far more likely to find the drainage conspicuous by its absence, the difficulties and obstacles of a kind that have to be removed at a considerable cost, the grass deficient both in quantity and quality. On inland courses you generally have to sod your putting greens, you certainly have to cut your bunkers, and you are fortunate if you do not find it necessary to root out a hundred acres of virgin forest. Even so, the battle is but half over.

A steam roller must be purchased to remedy the effects of a severe winter's frost, and in the west, at least, a water system which will cost you upwards of $5,000 under the most favorable circumstances, is absolutely essential to the proper enjoyment of the game. Add to this the minor fact that in the summer months you will probably run over the entire course with close cutting mowing machines, and you will have some conception of what it costs to purchase and keep links in America in first rate condition.

Necessary Expenditure

By this enumeration of expenses I do not mean to strike terror into the hearts of any struggling green committee who would disband at of a Good House. Once if such a sum as $100,000, or even a tenth part of it, were declared to be the minimum basis of calculations. If your aims are modest, you may start your golfing career on a much smaller capital; you may lay out a nine hole course to begin with, and be content to make your improvements very slowly. My intention is simply to point out that unless you are very favorably situated, as you might be, for instance, on Long Island, where the soil is sandy and bunkers are natural, you cannot get an eighteen hole course into first class condition in the short space of two or three years, and at the same time build and maintain a suitable club house without an outlay which will involve the expenditure of a sum very little short of $100,000.

The Advantages of a Good House

The club house, it may be remarked in passing, is a very necessary part of the scheme; for in order to get the required list of members it is necessary before anything else to supply those ordinary comforts and luxuries which will make up to the influential member for the tribulation that he goes through in trying to learn a game which he has not yet begun to love for its own sake. The history of golf clubs in this country is a constant repetition of the same story in that respect. The club is generally started by the enthusiastic few who want to play the game. In order to attain their ends they inveigle a number of their companions into subscribing for the purchase of the house and ground. There is no question about the loyalty of these laymen if they can only be induced to give the game a fair trial.

But there is always a period of trepidation when they have learned to complain to the house committee, but have not yet become interested in their scores to the exclusion of every other interest in life. Somewhere in his philosophical writings Mr. Punch tells a young wife that the best way to deal with a husband is simply to feed the brute. I would not go so far as that in plainness of speech, but I do consider it most important for the welfare of a new golf club, that those members whose subscriptions are desirable and whose golfing enthusiasm is not yet fully developed, should be brought into the fold by a nice regard for their personal comforts.

Taking everything into consideration, then, I hardly think that I have overestimated the sum which a new club must spend before it possesses a first class course. Whether that sum should be spent at once, or spread over a number of years, is entirely a matter for the committee upon ways and means to decide. The main thing to be desired is that the members of the club should not shut their eyes to the facts of the case. For if they are misled into thinking" that they can obtain the required results in a less expensive way, they are not only deceiving themselves, but they will probably waste a large amount of money in half measures; Work slowly if you will, but always keep the main end in view, so that whatever improvements you do decide upon may have a permanent value.

The Scarcity of Good Courses

The enormous cost of making of and maintaining a fine course in America is probably accountable for the fact that good courses are very few and far between. There is, perhaps, another reason; and that is the fact that country clubs were in existence before golf was ever mentioned, and when the new pastime was introduced the country clubs had to make the best of the property at hand, instead of looking for the most suitable natural location. Shinnecock Hills is one of the few sites for a golf club which seems to have been chosen with an eye to the best possibilities of the game. Other spots have been selected either because they were close to already existing clubs, or because they were within easy reach of the great cities. As a result there is not a single course in America which really compares with the best links in Great Britain. And the sooner we acknowledge that fact the better it will be for the game in this country. Where we generally make a mistake is in believing that an inland course can ever be made the equal of a North Berwick or St. Andrews.

Not that I would in any way detract from the praise due to the skill and energy which have been displayed in the laying out of some of our best links. Here, at all events, we have one of the important features of the development of golf on this side of the Atlantic.

In Great Britain there is no such thing as an inland course which in any way approaches perfection, the reason being that there are so many seaside links within easy reach that the improvement of those situated away from the sea is hardly worth the expense. Here we certainly have inland courses which infinitely surpass anything of the same nature in Great Britain, and what is far more to the point really present a first class test of golf. Visitors to America from the home of golf in Scotland have often expressed surprise at the wonderful way in which natural difficulties have been overcome. And since most of our courses must of necessity be removed from the sea, it is most gratifying to observe the great improvement which has taken place in a very short space of time. But, nevertheless, it is necessary to keep the ideal constantly in view, and to remember that with the best intentions in the world we still fall very far short of perfection.

The Inferiority of inland Courses

There are two respects in which inland courses must always, humanly speaking, fall short of the natural seaside links, and especially those which, like Prestwick, Sandwich and Machrihanish to name only three out of a very large number have been singularly favored by Providence. The turf on the inland course may be as good as possible, but it will never yield that fine quality of putting which makes the short game on the great courses so interesting.

Seaside grass is a thing entirely *sui generis*; it is the only grass which presents that smooth billiard table surface, so familiar to old golfers. On inland putting greens the turf may be so excellent that there is never any excuse for missing a put of two yards; but the ball travels in a different way; it never trickles from the club into the hole as the ivory trickles into the pocket of a billiard table. And that is where the real science of putting is exhibited. The man who is accustomed to play on well kept inland putting greens is sure to find himself hopelessly at sea when he comes to play over the genuine golfing turf, where the ball must be struck with the most delicate touch.

Secondly, it is practically impossible to reproduce by artificial means the great sand bunkers which are peculiar to the coast of Great Britain. It is just conceivable that such bunkers might be constructed inland, but the expense would be so enormous that the possibility may well be ignored.

And so the awe inspiring effect of a large sand bunker stretching for a hundred yards or more in front of the tee, and rising very often to the height of an ordinary house, is unknown to those who play only on inland courses, where bunkers are nothing but inconsiderable trenches, very ruinous, perhaps, to a score, but quite devoid of any power to destroy the nerve of the poorest player. I have often heard complaints made against the number of bunkers upon our best courses; and yet the fact is that there is not a single course in this country which has one third of the number of sand bunkers which may be encountered at St. Andrews, and not one whose bunkers piled all together would make a hazard of the dimensions of "the Maiden" at Sandwich or the "Himalayas" at Prestwick.

For that reason it will be readily under stood that there is less distinction here between a first class and a second class player than in Great Britain; for the character of the courses is such that innumerable drives may be missed without any serious penalty. Even where there are regular bunkers in front of the tee, they are so small that they only catch a few out of the many bad shots which are played. It may be argued, of course, that the same remark applies to St. Andrews, where it is possible to top at least twelve out of your eighteen tee shots and yet go unscathed.

But then, St. Andrews is perhaps the only first class course where such a state of things exists, and there are so many compensations in the shape of scattered bunkers through the course, and the holes are laid out so perfectly in the matter of distance, that the one failing is not so serious as it might be.

The Remedies

There are two ways of getting over the bunker difficulty on inland courses; neither of them is altogether satisfactory, but both may be employed with advantage. To begin with, whether your bunkers are large enough or not, it is always well to arrange your holes at such distances apart that a bad drive will be of necessity punished, whether it lands the ball in a hazard or not. Secondly, it is always possible, in summer, at least, to let the grass grow for about a hundred yards in front of the tee, so that a topped ball cannot run very far, and the second shot will in all likelihood be spoiled. The only objection to this plan is that it becomes monotonous, and also tends to a great loss of balls. If it has to be resorted to, the grass should be kept carefully cut to such an extent that the ball cannot very well run through it for any distance, and yet will not be entirely concealed from view.

For every other reason except to punish bad driving, long grass is a thing to be strenuously avoided in the fair course. It is a certain cause for the loss of valuable gutta percha, and therefore for the wasting of much more valuable time.

Method of Dealing with Inland Courses

Having once settled the question of the inferiority of all inland courses, we may proceed to the discussion of the means toward producing the best results with the material at hand.

Choice of Property

Begin by selecting the best soil that is available. Light, sandy soil is the best for the purpose, because it dries easily after rain, and yet does not bake to the consistency of iron in hot weather. A clay soil is strongly to be avoided. If you cannot get sand, search for rich loam, which is not so desirable either in drought or in rain, but yet affords a fine deep sod. If possible get a piece of property devoid of trees.

One of the constant incumbrances upon American courses is to be found in the shape of woodland. The desire to obtain picturesque surroundings has generally overruled more utilitarian motives, and so a budding golf club often invests in real estate which is quite unfit for the exercise of the game without an enormous expenditure of capital.

Removal of Obstacles

When you have bought your Obstacles, land, which should be as undulating as possible, without being mountainous, proceed to lay out the best course that the lie of the ground permits, irrespective of a building site for your club house or the picturesque grouping of woods. Then go to work ruthlessly and root out every tree which interferes in the most remote degree with your course. Remember that the course should be nearly seventy five yards wide at all points, and that there should not be a single tree of any description upon it. You will have to come to this state of things sooner or later; so you may just as well harden your heart at the beginning. You will probably encounter a good deal of antagonism from artistic souls, and will have to enjoy the reputation of utter vandalism; but that need not trouble you greatly. Your reward will come when the course is in a finished state, and in the meantime anyone who desires to indulge in amateur forestry can retire to some region which not been devoted to the ends of golf.

The Location of Holes

In laying out your holes do not be bound down by any cast iron rule. The distances on the best courses abroad have not been decided by regulation, but by the natural fitness of things. Of course, if your property consists simply of an expanse of more or less level pasture and that is, perhaps, the most promising material to work upon you can arrange the length of your holes to suit yourself. But in most cases there will be one or two special features which should be utilized in order to make picturesque holes, such as may differentiate your course from any other. It is not a bad plan to select your short hole first.

The most perfect kind of short hole is one which requires an iron shot on to a green where the flag is full in view, with a yawning hazard which stretches from the tee right up to the edge of the putting green. You will probably find such a hazard, or the opportunity for one, somewhere on your property, and you should choose that for one at least of your short holes. And then as a general rule look out for high spots and locate your putting greens there.

A links is made particularly interesting where you have the flag plainly visible from the teeing ground. There should be few, if any, blind holes upon a good course. Moreover, one advantage of having putting greens upon the high places is the fact that some of your teeing grounds will also of necessity be on eminences commanding a view of the entire ground over which you have to play. There is nothing prettier in golf than the play from a teeing ground on the top of a hill, with a large bunker immediately in front. If, therefore, your property possesses any special features of this kind, do not fail to make use of them even if you have on that account to depart from the actual distances sanctioned by custom.

Wherever your putting greens are not clearly determined for you by nature, you should have the ideal course constantly in view, and although you may show certain individuality in striving after it, its services as a rough basis are invaluable.

The Distances

The nearest approach to perfection in the matter of distances was made by the original founders of the St. Andrews links in Scotland. A plan of the course, with the correct distances, will be found at the end of this chapter; there are also diagrams of Prestwick and North Berwick, with the distances as nearly correct as is possible, in view of the fact that the teeing grounds vary considerably. Study Standers carefully, and you will discover that the holes are so distributed as to demand skill in every conceivable kind of stroke, and also to do away as far as possible with the element of luck.

St. Andrews

First of all, there are two short holes which vary, according to weather, between a full cleek shot and a half iron. Secondly, there are two holes, the ninth and the tenth, where the drive need only be followed by a very short approach. More than two such holes on an eighteen whole course must be avoided, because they allow the player to miss his drive very badly without any punishment whatsoever. It is rather a mistake to have holes of such a distance that a missed drive may be redeemed by a fine brassey shot; but it is a great deal worse when the difference between a good and a bad drive. Only entails the difference between a long iron approach and a short one. Still, two holes of the objectionable length from two hundred to three hundred yards are perfectly admissible in a full eighteen whole course, provided that the other distances are good. Now, at St. Andrews there are two five hundred yard holes, two of four hundred, and ten between four hundred and three hundred.

The long holes require two long drives and an approach, or three fair drives, the two of four hundred call for two very long shots with a wooden club, and the rest may be reached in two shots which vary between two full drive sand a drive followed by a half iron shot. In every case, with the exception of the ninth and tenth holes already alluded to, the tee shot must be clean hit not because there is a bunker to be negotiated, but because even a slight error will make it very hard, if not impossible, to reach the putting green with the second shot. It requires no extended argument to show that this is one of the most important points to bear in mind when laying out a new course; for it creates at once a wide distinction between the first class and the second class player.

Do not imagine, however, that your holes must really be of such a uniform character as this description might seem at first sight to imply. Although there are fourteen holes at St. Andrews which under ordinary circumstances may be reached in two strokes, and cannot be reached in less, the second stroke is probably a different one in every case. It may either be a very long shot with a wooden club or a full cleek shot, or a full iron or a half shot.

There are other ways, moreover, of varying the monotony by the arrangement of bunkers, and the situation of the putting greens. The second shot may have to be of the high or lofted variety so as to carry a bunker close to the hole, or it may be more advisable to play a running shot when there is no obstacle in the direct line, and the putting green is of such a nature as to make a lofted shot almost impossible.

Such is the case very often at North Berwick, where the hole is situated upon a hard plateau so that a ball pitched right on to the green is certain to run past the hole.

This, then, is the first principle to observe in selecting distances: Place your holes so far apart that, with only one or two exceptions, they can be reached in one, two or three full shots. As you will see by the diagram and figures, there are two holes at St. Andrews which may be reached easily in one stroke, two which may be reached in one and a little more; twelve that require two good shots, and two that can only be reached by the average good player in three; and after all, you cannot improve upon that as a basis for imitation.

Other Courses

Prestwick not being laid out as St. Andrews is, with parallel courses out and in r has a different arrangement. There is only one short hole the second of the regulation type. The fifth and the seventh are both short in the sense that they can be reached in one stroke, but on calm days they call for the use of a wooden club. There are two holes of the objectionable length, the sixteenth. And the eighteenth, both of which need only a drive and a very short approach; But there is this to be said in their favor, that a really long driver may get within putting distance off the tee, and in the case of the sixteenth, there are several bunkers to be avoided, so that a good drive is really very necessary.

A course of this nature has not the uniform perfection of St. Andrews, for its three short holes occur on the outward journey, making the first half round easier than the second. On the other hand, there is this objection to the St. Andrews course that the short, easy holes come in succession instead of being dispersed over the round. Sandwich is rather like Prestwick, except that the hazards are even more formidable. There are two short holes in the first half round which may be reached in one stroke. These are the sixth and the eighth perhaps the best short holes in existence except for the fact that they are both blind holes.

The eighth hole resembles the fifth at Prestwick in that it usually entails the use of a driver to surmount the tremendous bunker, which is well named Hades. Besides these short holes there are two, the third and the fifth, which may very nearly be reached in one good drive, and the second only requires a short approach; so that the outward journey is comparatively easy from the point of view of distance. The length of the carries, however, makes up for the deficiency in the total distance, and only very excellent play will account for a score below forty for the first nine holes. In the second half round there are two easy holes, the eleventh and the sixteenth, but the rest are long enough to balance the shortness of the first nine, and it is almost as easy to go below forty for the first half round as it is to improve upon forty five for the second. It is better, perhaps, if possible, to distribute your distances evenly between the two half rounds, but the natural lie of the ground must be considered as well, and I doubt very much whether the present course at Sandwich could be improved upon anywhere in the world.

The turf upon some of the courses in the west of Scotland is better, and the distances at St. Andrews are more perfect. But there is something about the enormous hazards and the constant variety of the great South of England course which makes it a source of infinite joy to the good player, even if it is less popular among the weaker brethren. In laying out an eighteen whole course you may imitate any one of these three links with advantage.

For a nine hole course, take St. Andrews and copy either the outward or the inward holes; there is very little difference between them in point of length; only you will have to alter the arrangement of your holes so as not to have the three shortest in succession.

The Improvement of the Ground

When once your distances are settled, you may set to work upon the ground itself. Hazards may be inserted at any time, and it is rather a mistake to cut up the ground hurriedly before you know exactly where your bunkers are required.

Rolling

Your first object should be to get the turf all through the course in perfect condition. If your land has been lying fallow for several years, your grass is probably sufficiently strong to stand a heavy steam roller. You will find it less expensive to invest in the machine at once rather than waste time and money in working with a horse roller, which, in wet weather, does almost as much harm as it does well. Seaside courses and those which are situated in temperate climates, hardly require such drastic treatment.

But on most of the inland courses of America which suffer from the severe frosts in winter, a steam roller will be found invaluable. From three to five tons is the best weight, and the width of the roller should be as great as possible. Roll the whole course as soon as the frost is fairly out of the ground, but beware against repeating the process too often. One good rolling in the spring ought to last a whole season.

Grass Cutting

As soon as your grass begins to grow you will find it impossible to keep it under control, if your soil is at all rich, without the help of a mowing machine. Most courses must be shaved close at least once a week during the early summer months, and that entails a considerable amount of labor. But there is no other way of meeting the difficulty. Of all faults in a links there is none more aggravating and more conducive to the ruin of the game than long grass in the regular course. It is only excusable in front of the tee to punish a topped drive, and even there it should be kept short enough to avoid a waste of time in looking for balls. Sheep are often recommended for the purpose of keeping the grass down; but no quantity of them will have a visible effect on an inland course in June, provided that your grass is in a healthy condition.

And sheep are such a nuisance in other ways that it is better to give them up entirely, and rely upon your lawn mowers. Possibly you may lose thereby in the matter of revenue, but it must always be remembered that golf and husbandry are distinct pursuits.

The Putting Greens

If your turf must be in perfect condition through the ordinary course, much more must your putting greens be flawless. If possible they should be made out of the original sod, with all the natural undulations intact. In many cases, however, it is necessary to relay them with fresh turf; and if that is done, great care should be exercised in order that they may not be absolutely flat and square. Nothing adds so much to the enjoyment of the game as a certain variety in the shape and contour of the different greens. Some should be on high ground, others in hollows.

A few should be on the side of hills, provided that the slope is very gentle; an occasional plateau may be selected, but in that case the green should not be too small. In size they should vary, but they should never have a radius of less than forty feet.

Mowing Machines

The excellence of your putting greens depends, to a large extent, upon the kind of mowing machine you possess. The ordinary Philadelphia lawn mower of common use does not cut the grass close enough for golfing purposes, and so it is necessary to have a special machine made, with the same width of blade but with smaller wheels, so that the knife may be brought closer to the ground. This slight change in the implement will make all the difference between good and bad putting greens.

Water

Finally, you must have a water supply available at each green. The actual amount of water to be used varies, of course, with the differences in climate. But there are very few parts of the United States where nature's water supply may not be supplemented with considerable advantage, and there are a great many regions where golf is out of the question on any other terms. In making your plans for a complete water system, there is only one thing to remember.

Green committees are apt to take an average rainfall as their basis, and imagine that four inches a month which would be a large allowance from heaven in any climate is more than sufficient when supplied by artificial means. One inch a week would certainly be ample for the purpose if it were distributed in cloudy weather, just as nature gives her moisture. But an artificial supply is only needed in warm, dry weather, when the evaporation is tremendous.

Consequently, what would be acceptable from nature will not nearly answer the purpose when it comes from a well. What you actually need depends entirely upon your climatic conditions. But it may be useful to point out that on courses in the west it is not at all too liberal to calculate upon a basis of half an inch a day during July and August. That, of course, is for the putting greens alone.

Generally speaking, no attempt is made to water the whole course. And yet there is no reason why even this task should not be undertaken in regions where golf is almost entirely ruined by the drought of the western summer. Granted that your water system is adequate for the purpose of keeping your putting greens in good condition, it would require no great expenditure to increase the supply and so be in a position to sprinkle your whole course once or even twice a week.

Of course the sprinkling must be a thorough one, to have the desired effect, but there are numberless courses west of the Alleghenies which would be improved five hundred per cent in the hot weather by the outlay.

In fact, an entirely satisfactory water system would make the whole difference between playing golf and playing some other inferior game. I do not imagine that there is any course in the east which requires this hydrogenic treatment; yet even there a good supply of water can do no harm, and will very often prove enormously beneficial.

Hazards

It only remains to speak of the various hazards which may be inserted in a course when the turf has been put in perfect condition. Once more let me repeat that all obstructions, such as trees, ditches, boulders and quarries, so often spoken of with pride as natural hazards, should at all costs be removed. The ideal way to go about making an inland links is to get; first of all, about two hundred acres of undulating pasture land without a single obstruction or excrescence of any sort.

There is, as a matter of fact, no such thing as a natural hazard upon an inland course, unless it is a stream or a pond of water. Having got your wide stretch of turf, which should be as smooth as velvet in every part, you may then put in all the sand bunkers you require; for sand bunkers are the only hazards, with the exception of water, which should be allowed under any circumstances. Long grass may grow off the course to punish wild driving, and in some cases it may be left, as explained above, in front of the tee. In cutting your bunkers do not be afraid to make them large and varied in shape.

Most inland greens are spoiled by the fact that the hazards are not big enough to catch all the missed balls which go in their direction. Do not forget, moreover, that in many cases the hazard should stretch from the edge of the teeing ground to a distance of a hundred yards or more, so that a missed drive must positively bring its punishment. A bunker is very little good unless it is thirty feet wide, or is guarded by a high face.

Whenever you see a ball jump a bunker which lies across the line of fire, you may take note of it, and if the same accident repeats itself often, you should set to work at once and widen your bunker. In making your hazards it is best to choose spots which are naturally suited to the purpose, such as hollows in the ground or hillsides; a regular line of cops set down on a flat surface present the appearance of military earthworks and add neither to the beauty of the landscape nor the variety of the game. In guarding your putting greens, do not always put a straight bunker right in front of the man who is approaching. Some greens should be protected in that way, others should be between hazards, a few should be entirely surrounded, and hardly any should be absolutely free. It is a good plan also to have at least one or two holes where the bunkers are so close that the approach must be played with a certain amount of back spin.

On most American courses the greens are either so small or keen that no mortal man can pitch his ball on them and keep it there, or else they are so large and free from bunkers that the veriest duffer can loft on to them with ease. The happy medium has not yet been struck. Of course every green should not be too closely guarded, but a few out of the eighteen should certainly call for a display of skill in administering back spin. And in order to bring about this end, your greens must be keen.

Provided that your water supply is adequate and your grass is strong it is quite impossible to make an inland green too keen. As long as you keep your turf watered every night in warm weather, you may cut the grass as short as possible, and yet not make your putting and approaching too difficult. The expense of making bunkers on inland courses is naturally large. For that reason it is particularly desirable that you should go boldly to work at first upon your hazards and make them of a proper size. A bunker thirty feet wide will stop most topped balls, but that is practically the minimum. Many of them should be considerably larger.

Summary

These, then, are the main thing's to bear in mind, and I may repeat them shortly as follows: For the purpose of making" an eighteen hole course, look out first for at least two hundred acres of the best pasture land, provided that you cannot get the genuine golf land by the sea. Avoid a clay soil. Make your course seventy five yards wide at every hole and remove every tree, ditch and stone from its surface.

Locate your putting" greens first with regard to natural situation, and then model your distances upon the St. Andrews links in Scotland. Roll your course every spring, and keep it close cut with mowing machines in summer. Make your putting greens as perfect as the abundant use of water and the mowing" machine will permit Let all your hazards be sand bunkers, with the addition of a water hazard if nature supplies it. Make your bunkers large and varied in shape you cannot make them too large and guard all your putting greens either on one or upon every side.

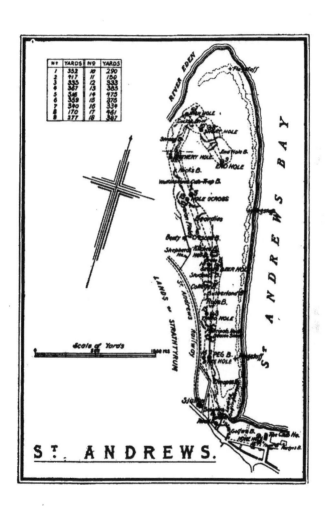

Nº	YARDS	Nº	YARDS
1	352	10	290
2	417	11	150
3	335	12	333
4	367	13	385
5	348	14	475
6	359	15	275
7	340	16	334
8	170	17	461
9	277	18	387

RIVER EDEN

Fog Point

ST. ANDREWS BAY

LANDS OF STRATHTYRUM

St Andrews Railway

Scale of Yards

ST. ANDREWS.

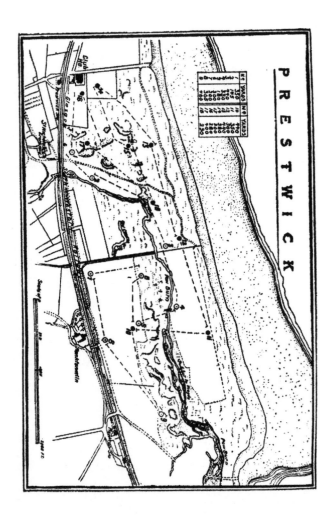

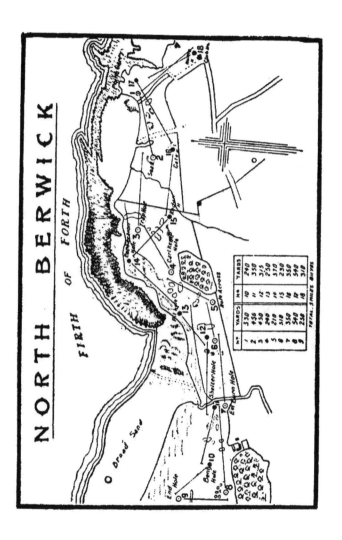

NORTH BERWICK

FIRTH OF FORTH

Nº	YARDS		Nº	YARDS
1	330		10	240
2	456		11	350
3	430		12	315
4	240		13	250
5	210		14	370
6	310		15	230
7	350		16	350
8	540		17	540
9	230		18	310

TOTAL 5 MILES 80 YDS

CHAPTER VIII
DEVELOPMENT OF THE GAME IN AMERICA

If the courses on this side of the Atlantic fall far short of perfection, it must still be remembered that they are situated for the most part in regions where the average Briton would have despaired of ever making golf a possibility; and yet they do, in many cases, present a very fair test of the game.

The Improvement of Inland Courses

And so the apotheosis of the inland course maybe regarded as one of the great features of the development of golf in America up to the present time. The genius of the American people is naturally inclined toward haste and impatience. That is why so many links in this country have been laid out in such a way that they will have to be entirely remodeled from the very beginning before they can rank in the first class.

On the other hand, when the true idea of the game is thoroughly grasped, there is no obstacle great enough to prevent speedy success in the perfecting of the unpromising material at hand. If New York and Chicago were suddenly transported to the desert of Arabia, I have not a doubt that they would in the space of twelve months be surrounded by a circle of excellent golf courses. You have, as a rule, merely to point out to an American Green Committee that a certain thing is necessary, and you may count upon getting it.

And for that reason we have inland courses in America which come within measurable distance of some of the best seaside links.

The Governing Body

The organization of the game is also a peculiarity of its growth in the States. Golf has been played in Scotland from time immemorial, and yet there has never been a governing body which has had anything more than a prescriptive right to control the national laws and practice of the game. The committee of the Royal and Ancient Club at St. Andrews has gradually assumed the reins of government, not from any desire to usurp authority, but simply because no other method of control seemed practicable. If there had been as many clubs in England twenty five years ago as there were in Scotland, and if the interest in the game had been at all evenly distributed, there would have been no difficulty in instituting some kind of national administration. But as it was, there were few good players in Great Britain who were not members of the Royal and Ancient Golf Club, and it would have been manifestly absurd, or at least very unnecessary, to suggest that the St. Andrews committee was not perfectly competent to do all that was required in the way of government. Moreover, national associations have never been recognized as the ruling principle of English sport.

The government of the game of golf having been gradually thrust upon the St. Andrews club, it grew more and more impossible to organize any national committee in the face of the conservative element. The case of the Marylebone cricket club was cited to support the rule of a single club as against the control of a national association. And so, in one way and another, the constitution of the game as it at present exists became crystallized. A step in the direction of a national committee was made some ten years ago when the Hoylake Club instituted the amateur championship tournament, but the time had gone by when the organization of such a committee upon democratic lines was possible. In the first place, only a few of the many clubs in the country were represented; and secondly, the delegates sent to choose the course for the decision of the next championship, were powerless to assume authority upon any other subject.

And so, for better or for worse, the Standers Club has become the M. C. C. of golf, and all hopes of a general committee seem at present exceedingly remote except, indeed, on such terms as would rob the institution of half its value as a representative body. It must not be imagined for a moment by those who know golf only as it is played in America that this apparently hap hazard kind of government has been detrimental to the development of the game.

There are two distinct sides to the question; and it may be asserted with great safety that the game would have suffered enormously in the past if the influence of St. Andrews had not been predominant.

There is no game in the world which admits of so much ignorance upon the part of its players as golf. And if, ten or fifteen years ago, men who had only pursued the gutta percha in the wilds of Tooting-Bec or the Cowley marshes at Oxford had been allowed the same vote in the control of the game as the first class players of St. Andrews, the results would have been most disastrous.

At the same time, golf has now reached a point in England and Scotland, where the mists of ignorance have been widely dissipated, and the moment has arrived when the formation of a national association would in all probability be most beneficial. But in the meantime St. Andrews has the power, and why should she relinquish it?

Philanthropic bimetallists are fond of asking England to abandon her gold standard. Those who make a similar request of St. Andrews find themselves in much the same predicament. Their theory is excellent, but what inducement have they got to offer?

There is the dilemma; and we have to thank our stars of good fortune that we had no such difficulty to face when the game became popular in America. The idea of the national association had become fixed in the minds of all sportsmen in this country by its success in other branches of athletics, and there was no traditional influence to overcome.

The United States Golf Association

On the other hand, there was a very serious danger that American players, with their half digested notions of golf and their knowledge of most inferior courses, should go about to make some very radical changes in the rules and practice of the game. In fact, a tendency in that direction was noticeable when a rule was made that a ball might be lifted and teed in match play as it may be in playing a medal competition.

THE LATE THEODORE A. HAVEMEYER
First President C S. G. A

Here at the outstart was a direct blow at the ruling principle of match play which is the real game of golf that the ball must be played wherever it lies, unless it be in water. The new rule has since been rescinded, and no farther attempt has been made to alter the St. Andrews rules as they stand. The only reason why this danger has been averted is that a national association was formed before any havoc could be created, and a committee elected, composed of men who had the best interests of the game at heart. The first president was the late Theodore A. Havemeyer, of whose services to golf and to amateur sport in general it is hard to speak dispassionately. It is seldom that a man of affairs, whose administrative powers have been developed in the control of a great corporation, is willing to devote a large share of his time and care to the interests of a game.

When this administrative ability is combined with the most lovable characteristics of a gentleman and a sportsman, it will be understood that the National Golf Association was extraordinarily fortunate in the selection of its first president. By his death, every golf player in this country sustained a great and irreparable loss. But in the two years of his control he was able to place the governing body upon so firm and immovable a basis, and his influence was so strong in preserving the true spirit of the game, that even his untimely departure could not spoil the complete value of his work.

There is but little doubt that had a weaker hand been at the helm during the young days of the association, many radical changes might have been made in the rules which would have made a gulf between the American and British golfers, and in the end might have been found entirely unnecessary. As it is, nothing has been done which could offend the most conservative spirit, nor is any action likely to be taken in the future which will bring about a development of the game along divergent lines in the two countries.

It would be beyond the scope of the present work to dwell upon the merits of the men who, as members of the executive committee, assisted Mr. Havemeyer in his good work; and yet one word must be said in passing recognition of the services done to golf in this country by Mr. Charles B. Macdonald, whose energy of purpose and fine instinct for the best points in the game have constituted him the arch pioneer of golf in America; by Mr. Henry O. Tallmadge, the most indefatigable of secretaries; by Mr. Laurence Curtis, whose clear judgment proved invaluable in preparing the new edition of the rules; and by Mr. Parrish, who would certainly be elected treasurer for life if he could only be induced to take the office.

MR. H. O. TALLMADGE
First Secretary U. S. G. A.

The attitude assumed by these men in the government of the association must have come in the way of a revelation to all British players, who are apt to have preconceived notions on the subject of American rashness and scorn for tradition. Not only has the spirit, but even the letter of the game been preserved with the most scrupulous care; and yet at the same time new suggestions have been admitted of such excellent propriety that even in the short space of three years American golfers have been able to offer hints upon which the more inert and less organized body of players in Great Britain will be compelled to act.

The Executive Committee of the U.S Golf
Association 1807

The Champion Tournaments

The conduct of the amateur championship meeting was the first instance of the advantage of bringing common sense to bear upon the subject. The system has still to undergo a slight revision before it can be called perfect, but the essential principles of the arrangement are incontrovertibly correct. The weeding out process is so simple that when it is once suggested, one wonders why it was never introduced before. Not only is it absolutely fair to everyone, but it requires that the champion shall show at least a certain skill in medal play, which, after all, is a department of the game. In the second place, it will obviate in large measure the luck of the draw. As things at present exist in Great Britain, a good player may go through one or two rounds without the slightest exertion, if he is fortunate in coming against weak opponents.

Under the American system he has to work for his position from the drop of the flag. He must play first class golf for two rounds of medal play in order to qualify at all, and then he will have to meet in each round a foeman who is worthy of his steel; for among the first sixteen who earn the right to compete there can be very few who have not a good chance of winning outright.

At least one or two changes will in all probability shortly be made in the rules of the contest. In the first place, all the match play rounds will consist of thirty six holes. Heretofore only eighteen holes were played, until the final round, and there was always a chance of a fluke victory; when every match is decided by playing thirty six holes, the element of luck is almost entirely eliminated.

Secondly, it is proposed in future to draw the first eight of the sixteen against the second eight for the first match play round, so that it will be impossible for a weak player to get into the finals; and also there will be a further inducement for the best players to return as good a card as possible. Upon this innovation I need not lay so much stress. It happens that at present in America there are not sixteen players of equal merit, and there is likely to be a difference of at least a third of a stroke a hole between the first and the last of the sixteen. In a year or two, however, the number of first class players will have increased so enormously that it will be impossible to name one of the first sixteen who has not a good chance of winning, and so the division of the draw would be unnecessary. But granted that the first of these improvements is determined upon, I cannot see how the arrangement of the contest can possibly be bettered.

The tournament will last five days, however large the entry maybe; all the bad players will be removed from the field after the first day; the winner must play five matches of thirty six holes each, including the preliminary medal round; there can be no possible chance of a lucky draw; and the man who finally becomes champion will have earned the title by sheer superiority of skill and endurance; So much for the amateur championship.

This means, of course, that the open event must be played on a separate occasion. So far that contest has been robbed of nearly all its interest by being thrown in, as it were, at the end of the tournament, which is manifestly hard upon the professionals, whose play, under the circumstances, attracts very little attention; and unfair to the amateurs, who cannot be expected to do themselves justice after the wear and tear of their own competition. It is only right, moreover, to remark, in passing, that American amateur form has been slightly discredited abroad for this very reason. In the championship tournament of 1897 the best amateur score was eleven strokes behind the winning score of 163 made by Lloyd; and it is argued by writers on the subject in England that the amateurs in America are therefore considerably behind amateurs in Britain on that account.

The fact is undoubtedly true, but not to the extent that the figures would show; simply because the amateurs in America have entered the open contest, up to the present time, merely as a matter of custom, without the slightest chance of displaying their best form. Lloyd's score of 163 was an exceedingly fine one, considering the length of the course; but it must be remembered that in the same week, under stress of greater heat, the first three returns for the Chicago cup were 81, 82 and 83, the latter score being made by Mr. J. A. Tyng, an American player of only three years' standing.

To be perfectly just to the professionals, I would say that only one or two of them show any superiority whatever over the best amateur form, and that both amateurs and professionals is from three to four strokes behind their colleagues on the other side of the Atlantic.

The Rules

To return from this digression, let us look for a moment at the question of the rules of the game. It is here that the American association has an enormous advantage over the governing body at St. Andrews. With all possible respect and love for the Royal and Ancient home of the game, I am constrained to assert, having the broad Atlantic between me and the 'niblicks' of those who will gain say me, that the various codes of rules sanctioned by the members of the club from time to time are monuments of judicial inefficiency. The fact is that the ordinary Scotch player who has been born and bred in the atmosphere of the game has no need of a written code at all. He plays the game by instinct and as the spirit guides him. That is precisely the reason why the old fashioned St. Andrews player was of necessity incompetent to draw up rules for the guidance of those who did not play by precedent rather than precept. What might be abundantly clear to him, knowing the practice and tradition would probably be most obscure to the Englishman and American. That this is the case has been proved conclusively by the voluminous rulings and interpretations made by Messrs. Ruther Ford and Lockyer; and yet their work left an enormous field for discussion upon points which they did not even touch. Of course it is impossible to make the rules of the game absolutely sufficient for the purpose; but there is a wide gulf between such a state of perfection and the condition of thing's as they now exist.

A careful study of the latest code of rules will convince any unprejudiced person that there are very few which, even to the experienced golfer, may not bear various meanings, and several which, if carried to their legitimate conclusion, are manifestly absurd. Fortunately the United States Golf Association has been able to issue a book of rulings and interpretations which does not altogether do away with the incongruities of the original code, but does at least settle a number of disputed points.

In Great Britain this course was out of the question because obviously the Royal and Ancient club, having issued its edict, could not, without appearing ridiculous, publish an explanation of the same. Messrs. Rutherford and Lockyer's work might have been of some assistance, but it was without authority, and could not really be quoted in defense of any argument. The United States Golf Association was very careful not to alter a single word in the text of the St. Andrews rules, and in this respect they acted very wisely.

The interpretations in many cases answer the purpose of a new rule, and in the meantime we may hope for a new and better code from the committee which has recently been appointed by the Royal and Ancient Golf Club.

The Hazard Rule

A full discussion of the weaknesses of the rules as they exist would be neither possible nor desirable at present. But one example may be taken as the text of a few remarks upon the subject. The hazard rule as it stands is the worst of all the St. Andrews regulations. It may, of course, be interpreted in such an extreme way as to make the game ridiculous. But even when taken in the broadest and most legitimate sense, its provisions are so unfair that here the interpretation of the executive committee is tantamount to a new rule. According to the law as it stands by itself, any player who touches sand in a bunker while addressing the ball is disqualified in medal play. Consequently, supposing that a competitor for the amateur championship in America, or the open championship abroad, were blown over by a gust of wind while aiming at the ball, or should for any other reason rest his club inadvertently upon the sand, he would at once be removed from the contest.

Such a rule defeats its own ends, because it is never, as a matter of fact, adhered to, especially in the case of bent and gorse. The interpretation made by the association is probably as satisfactory as anything could be under the circumstances. But why should not the rule be altered and made simpler?

First of all, nothing but sand or loose earth should be regarded as a hazard. That, of course, was the original intention of the rule. It is only in sand or loose earth that the player can possibly obtain any unfair advantage by grounding his club, or by moving loose obstacles. There is no possible reason why a loose stone should not be removed when the ball is lying in a gorse bush if it is allowable to remove one in the fair green. There is a very definite reason why a similar obstacle should not be removed in a bunker; because it is impossible to say in many cases where stones become small enough to be considered part of the sand. But on a good links there should be no stones whatever in any hazard, so that the break club question need hardly arise.

First of all, then, confine your hazards to sand and loose earth, and you will not only simplify matters, but you will be conforming in reality with the true spirit of the game. Secondly, make it a case for disqualification, or the loss of the hole, when a player deliberately removes anything in a bunker within a given radius of his ball. If a man is foolish enough to break the rules in a deliberate way, he deserves any punishment which may be meted out to him. But for grounding the club unintentionally or intentionally behind the ball in the act of addressing it the penalty of a stroke is quite sufficient.

No one, however expert he may be, can calculate upon improving the lie of his ball in addressing it sufficiently to warrant the loss of a stroke, and the rule about intentional removal of obstacles would still prevent him from deliberately scraping away the sand with his club. A rule written on these lines would provide ample punishment for carelessness, and it would also guard against the success of those players and there are a few of them who are always anxious to take every inch of rope that the law will concede. This is only one case out of a great many where it is easy to suggest a good rule where the founders of the code seem to have gone out of their way to make a bad one. Instances might be multiplied if necessary. My main object at present is to show what advantages may accrue from the government of an executive committee which is entirely national in its interests, which is not hampered by any uncertainty about its authority or any traditions of the past, and which, above all, is a thoroughly representative body. The members of the executive committee are chosen not with reference to the club they represent, but on account of their personal fitness. There is only one criticism to be made upon the constitution of the association, and that applies to the distinction between allied and associate members, a distinction which seems to have no very good raison d?2tre,and will in all probability be removed in the near future.

Club Matches

There is another development of the game in this country in the direction of increased interest in club matches, which has both advantages and disadvantages. Golf has never been regarded as a game for team matches in the past; it never can, from the very nature of things, be regarded in that light in the future. There is absolutely no scope for team work in these encounters between clubs, and so, at best, they can only be taken as an excuse for friendly gatherings.

Looked at from that point of view, they are entirely unobjectionable, and very often most enjoyable. Yet there is a certain danger in them, especially in America, which, however slight, ought to be carefully guarded against. So far golf, both here and in Great Britain, has been free from any taint of semi professionalism; and very naturally so, because it has always been regarded as a game for individual amusement. Amateur championships are inventions of recent date, and club matches would probably never have crept into practice if it had not been for the inter university contests at Oxford and Cambridge. It is easily understood that where a man plays for his own amusement the element of semi professionalism cannot exist; but as soon as club rivalry is introduced the inducement to resort to questionable methods becomes a factor in the game. It is very hard for golfers in England and Scotland to understand that such a danger can exist, because they have never looked upon club rivalry as a determining feature of the situation.

Here in America the spirit of competition is so keen in every walk of life that it is just as well to face the danger at the outset and make provision against it; for it would be a thousand pities if the disease which has infected both football and baseball should spread into golf.

The Benefit of Better Courses

Possibly the best way of dealing with the subject is for the association to take absolutely no cognizance of club matches ; in that way the club match may still be a source of enjoyment without becoming a matter of public interest. And in the second place, I am confident that the gradual improvement in the various courses all over the country will make golf more and more desirable for its own sake, and not for the glory or rewards which at present give it a spurious value. There is not a doubt that inferior courses lead to a multiplying of competitions of every kind, because interest must be stimulated in every way to make up for the defects in the game itself. It is an invariable rule that the better the links the fewer are the competitions. This argument applies not only to the hunting after prizes, but in a minor degree to club matches. If your course is a good one you will get far more enjoyment out of a week's good match plays than from any number, of official events.

CHAPTER IX
AMATEURS ABROAD

There have been so many discussions of a somewhat futile nature upon the relative merits of British and American players that it may be interesting to know exactly how golfers in America rank with the experts on the other side of the water. As I have already pointed out, the conclusions which might be drawn from the results of the amateur and open competitions held in this country during the last three years are manifestly unfair to the amateurs, for the very simple reason that the amateurs have never yet met the professionals on even terms. And had they done so, it must be remembered that Lloyd's score of 163 at Wheaton in the championship tournament of 1897 compares very favorably with the winning scores over such courses as Hoylake and Muirfield, which are certainly two strokes easier than the course of the Chicago golf club; and it is not so many years ago that no amateur in Great Britain was expected to come within ten strokes of the first place in the open event.

As far as I can judge, it is impossible to compute the difference between first class form here and in Scotland or England by a definite number of strokes. The class in America is so exceedingly small that the results attained are, comparatively speaking, most indifferent. And yet the class exists and must be judged on its merits.

The difference really consists only in the matter of steadiness and confidence in tournament play. Mr. Charles Macdonald may be taken as a typical example of the first class American amateur. His record for a single season over the links of the Chicago Golf Club at Wheaton is almost as good as that of any Scotch player over the links of St. Andrews. And yet in tournament play he would certainly be outclassed by the first six or eight amateurs who are sure to put in an appearance for any great event in Scotland. It may seem strange that a player, who is capable of producing an invincible game on ordinary occasions, should fail when skill is most called for. In reality the explanation is very simple.

No one who has lived in America up to the present time can possibly have acquired the tournament habit; for after all, the ability to play up to form in important events is not entirely a matter of nerve, but comes in great measure from long experience; and as important tournaments have only recently been instituted in America such experience is entirely out of the question. The only difference between the first class proper in Great Britain, and the much larger class which includes the rank and file of those who are placed at scratch in the handicap list of the Royal and Ancient Golf Club, lies in the possession of this same tournament habit; and it is exceedingly rarely that any very young player makes his way into the real aristocracy of the game.

Even when he does he is not by any means sure to keep his position, as is proved by the fact that Mr. P. C. Anderson, one of the youngest of amateur champions, has failed to live up to the honors that he won a few years ago. Mr. F. G. Tait was considered a mere boy when he captured the coveted laurels in1896; but he was twenty five years of age, and had also had the advantage of constant familiarity with the best players from the time that he first went to school. The real first class in Great Britain is confined to those members of the big brigade who went down at Muirfield last spring before the prowess of two comparative youngsters in the persons of Mr. Robb and Mr. Allen. In spite of their defeat, they are still the leading figures in amateur golf, partly on account of their past career, and partly because they are sure to supply most of the medal winners and champions for some time to come.

The list includes the names of Mr. John Ball, Mr. J. E. Laidlay, Mr. Harold Hilton, Mr. F. G. Tait, Mr. Horace Hutchinson, Mr. Leslie Balfour Melville, Mr. Mure Fergusson and the Messrs. Blackwell. To these we must add, in view of recent events, the names of Mr. Allen and Mr. Robb.

Take these men and a few others, whom I may have inadvertently omitted, from the so called first class in Great Britain, and I do not think that there are any players out of the remainder who are likely to show better form than can be seen among the first class players of this country always provided that the term first class as applied to American golf really applies only to those who have learned their game in Scotland.

When we come to the average scratch player in American clubs, such as Mr. Fenn, Mr. Tyng, and a host of others who have shown skill in other branches of athletics, we are dealing with a different class altogether, composed of men who would rank for the most part with the converted cricketers of England, such as Mr. E. Buckland, Mr. C. Toppin, Mr. Croome and many others who have discarded the bat in favor of the driver. These players are rather better than the regular second class performers according to the old system of division when the second class included all those who could play Mr. Laidlay or Mr. Balfour Melville with a third of a stroke a hole.

The cricketing contingent can do better than that, and yet they are generally too unsteady to be classed even with the ordinary scratch players at St. Andrews. To put it shortly, then, I should place our first class proper on the same level as the average scratch players of St. Andrews, and our best native talent on a par with the cricketers in England. What the precise difference is between our first class proper and the British first class proper is still an uncertain quantity, but it depends a great deal upon the ability of men of the Ball and Hilton class to play their best game when it is most required. The existence of this special class in England and Scotland is only of recent date, and so we need not despair of making a similar advance in this country before many years is past.

The improvement in American golf courses is a most important factor in the development of the game; but of greater weight still is the fact that our college boys are only now beginning to take golf seriously. When they have had a few more years' practice the limits of our first class will be enormously extended; for youthful training alone can produce the very best players.

MR. J. E. LAIDLAY

Among those who belong to the inner circle in Great Britain there is no more brilliant and successful player than Mr. J. E. Laidlay. The only distinction which he has not won is the open championship of England and Scotland, and that is a prize which has only three times fallen to an amateur.

He has been amateur champion twice, and there is hardly a club of high standing in Scotland which does not claim him as a medal winner. Mr. Laidlay never, perhaps, attained that perfection of steadiness which for many years made Mr. John Ball almost invincible. On the other hand, he is accustomed to make so many extraordinary recoveries from seemingly hopeless situations that it has always been a great treat to watch his game in an important match.

Not only is he marvelously effective in a high wind a thing which in itself goes far to distinguish the really first-class player from the average scratch man, but he is one of the few men who seem able to do a hole of almost any length in three when circumstances require it. To a certain extent Mr. Laidlay had for a few years a deteriorating effect upon incipient golfers; because he was the first great player to adopt the method of driving off the left leg. For several years he had innumerable imitators who could easily assume a similar position, but never exhibited the genius necessary for making it successful. For a short time, indeed, it was more common to see examples of this style on the links than the older St. Andrews fashion.

The fad has had its day by this time, and it will be a long time, in all probability, before another first class player appears with so extreme a method. It may be equally long before we meet anyone who has so perfect a control over his iron clubs. The old course at North Berwick has been lengthened and improved beyond recognition, and so it will never again be possible to see Mr. Laidlay negotiating the many short holes which used to demand the utmost skill in iron play.

There was every kind of stroke then, from a full cleek to a mashie shot, and generally it was necessary to pitch the ball upon a keen sloping green surrounded by hazards. No one has ever surpassed Mr. Laidlay at this game, and it is doubtful whether anyone ever will surpass him. Mr. Ball's full cleek shots are a marvel to all beholders; Andrew Kirkcaldy can get as far with a half iron as most men can with a brassey, and Willie Campbell in his day was the greatest exponent of the mashie. But no player, either amateur or professional, has such a perfect command over every iron club in the set as Mr. Laidlay. As a driver he is brilliant, but inclined to be erratic on occasion, a fault which gives him ample opportunity of displaying his great power of recovery.

On the putting green he is also a trifle uncertain. Few men hole a greater number of long puts than he, and yet few among the first class players miss so many short ones. In this respect, at least, he is mortal, and that is possibly the reason that he has never won the open championship, which is decided by medal play.

Mr. Ball has won both the open and amateur championships, the latter upon four occasions, and is also so fine a match player that he must be ranked as the most successful, and indeed the greatest amateur golfer of the day. If he is more liable to defeat now than he was a few years ago, it must be remembered that general form has improved wonderfully of late, and it would be impossible for anyone to maintain for very long the unique position which he held in the golfing world a short time ago.

Of a slight but wiry frame, he is possessed of great physical strength and endurance. And here it may be well to remark upon the fact that the idea which many people still entertain regarding the amount of muscle requisite for pre eminence in the game is entirely erroneous. No one could call Mr. Ball, or Mr. Laidlay, or Mr. Hilton a physical giant; but they are all men of great muscular power and perfect health, accustomed to an abundance of outdoor exercise. Great height is not apparently of any particular advantage, although it is naturally conducive to long driving.

The Messrs. Blackwell, Mr. Arnold Blyth and Mr. Mure Fergusson, to mention no others, are instances of large, powerful men who excel in the use of the wooden club. But, after all, there is practically little difference between the driving of the most powerful player, and that of a man like Mr. Hilton, who is, comparatively speaking, of small stature. It is only in the case of Mr. "Ted" Blackwell that the added distance begins to tell.

MR. JOHN BALL

Certainly Mr. Ball is as fine a driver as anyone could wish to be, and he probably weighs less than Mr. Hilton. But then, he is a man of iron muscle, and that is the essential thing. A weak player may drive excellently for eighteen holes or so, but he is bound to tire sooner or later, especially when any strain is put upon him. Moreover, he is very apt to be short with his iron clubs. Mr. Ball and Mr. Hilton can drive just at well at the end of four days' tournament as at the beginning, because being naturally endowed with strength of limb; they always have something in reserve. No one seeing Mr. Hilton finishing his fourth round in the open event could ever imagine that he had exerted himself at all.

He never seems to drive a very long ball, and what is more curious, he generally drives rather high. Yet when the distance is actually measured he is just as likely to be ahead of a long driving opponent as not. It is in the short game that he is mostly to be feared. When the average scratch player holes a ball with his mashie at a distance of thirty or forty yards, the feat is looked upon as an egregious fluke, at least by his antagonists.

MR. HILTON AND MR. MURE-FERGUSSON

When Mr. Hilton takes up his mashie, you are never quite sure that he is not going to finish matters with one stroke until the ball stops rolling. In playing for the open championship at Muirfield, a few years ago, he twice holed the ball with his mashie in the last round, and once when he was lying almost buried in a rabbit scrape.

That, of course, was an extraordinary stroke of luck; but still it is not exaggeration to say that when he does get into the hole with a short approach shot, it is not always to be regarded as a mistake. One curious fact about Mr. Hilton's career is that he has twice won the open championship, but never has quite succeeded in winning the amateur event.

This inconsistency is generally laid down to his great steadiness and precision, which have a more telling effect in compiling a score than in match play. And yet his actual figures do not show this extraordinary steadiness. At Muirfield his last round was marvelously low, and so, too, he only succeeded in defeating Mr. F. G. Tait at Hoylake in 1897 by accomplishing the last eighteen holes in seventy five strokes. The fact remains, however, that he has twice defeated all comers in the open field, and that is sufficient glory to last any amateur a lifetime.

Photographed by R. W. Hawks, Edinburgh

MR. F. G. TAIT, DRIVING

Mr. Tait has come nearer equaling this feat than anyone else, because twice in succession he has been within an ace of securing the coveted position; so that, although he has never actually won the open championship, he has at least proved himself worthy of the highest rank. He has never won his spurs easily, for he had several hard fights for the amateur championship before he actually came to the front in 1896.

In nothing that he has done, therefore, has he been in any way indebted to fortune. In fact, there is no player at the present moment whose chances for any event would be reckoned higher than his. He won the St. Andrews medal at a very early age, but he had worked hard for the distinction. From his earliest years he was accustomed to play over the St. Andrews links, and when he first went to school he was in the habit of playing occasional matches with several of the leading amateurs; and that is a privilege which very few boys can enjoy.

Consequently his arrival at the top of the ladder was constantly expected, and in all human probability he is bound to stay there for many years to come. His aptitude for sports is another proof of the fact that few golfers ever reach the summit of their ambition that is not blessed with physical advantages. Mr. Tait was a good cricketer at school, and a first class football player at Sandhurst and what is still more important, there is not a fellow sportsman in any branch of athletics who knows him and familiarly calls him "Freddy," who has not also the greatest admiration for his good qualities. But of all golfers in the world the most popular is

Mr. Horace G. Hutchinson, who is just as well known by his writings as by his successes on the links. Mr. Hutchinson was, I suppose, the first Englishman who ever won the St. Andrews medal, and the mere fact that he could do such a thing, and still retain the friendship of Scotchmen, speaks volumes in his favor. When he first astonished the inhabitants of St. Andrews by the marvelous accuracy of his driving, he was one of the most dangerous men in any field. Since that time he has been a victim to the all devouring epidemic of influenza, and is no longer such a formidable member of the small band; but every now and then he gives the public a taste of his old quality, and when that is the case, the victory is sure to be a popular one. Few men are his superiors today on the field of battle; no one comes near him in the world of golfing literature.

From the time that he issued his first little work upon golf, which in itself was an epitome of what all such books should be, he has never failed of a large and enthusiastic audience. The Badminton book is almost entirely the work of his pen, and to day it is the only great classic upon the subject. Times have changed since it was first published, and yet there is very little of practical use to the golfer which he cannot find there today expressed in the most simple and readable language. Mr. Leslie Balfour Melville is another golfer who has been many years before the public. It would be unkind here to say how many years ago he first won the St. Andrews medal; and indeed, if I did hunt up the date in the book of the Royal and Ancient Golf

Club, no one after seeing him would believe it. Nothing could have been more gratifying than his victory in the amateur championship of 1895. Not only did it come as a well merited reward to one of the best athletes that Scotland has ever produced, but it served to show that none, or at least very few of us, need ever despair of developing a really first class game, even though we may have lived long on the shady side of thirty. Of course Mr. Balfour Melville had a great deal in his favor.

He has always been a successful golfer, and in addition has done more for Scotch cricket than any other player He also won laurels on the football field in his college days and is an expert in every game that he takes up. But that does not alter the astonishing fact that after ranking among first class golfers for nearly a quarter of a century he is still able to defeat young and old alike in the most important event of the year.

Of the other great players volumes might be written, but a few words must suffice here in passing tribute to the extra ordinary game which Mr. " Ted" Black well has developed and retained, in spite of many successive years spent on a ranch in California without any chance of wielding a golf club. Mr. Blackwell is, with the probable exception of Douglas Rolland, the only player of whom one can positively say that his driving is superior to that of the average first class golfer. There are several men who rank as exceptionally long drivers, but put them against Mr. Balfour Melville or Mr. Hilton, who has no such reputation and you, will find very little difference in the average distance. An occasional advantage of ten yards is really of very small value unless it is constant.

With Mr. Blackwell it is not a question of ten yards, but more generally thirty or forty; and that is heart breaking. There are many feats of driving which have been handed down to golfing history in illustration of Mr. Blackwell's prowess. The most remarkable is perhaps one which he accomplished at St. Andrews several years ago, when he drove the long hole at St. Andrews in two shots each way, thus proving that the wind had nothing to do with it.

On another occasion I saw him drive the wall hole at Prestwick in two shots three times on the same day. That this was an extraordinary performance may be judged from the fact that the actual distance which has to be covered is over four hundred yards, with a wall at the end of it, so that the roll of the second shot cannot be taken into consideration.

Moreover, the hole is only driven in two upon rare occasions when there is a strong wind in favor of the play. On this particular day Mr. Blackwell had no wind behind him to speak of; and twice out of the three times he used only an iron club for the second shot. That is the kind of driving that makes a difference. Mr. Blackwell is not above the average in his short game, but his driving is so magnificent that he can well afford a few missed puts. It would be peculiarly interesting to encounter Mr. Blackwell upon an American links, because either the climate here is in favor of long driving or American players drive an exceptionally long ball.

Last year Mr. McCawley, of the Philadelphia Country Club, won a long driving competition with a carry of two hundred and eight yards, and that with hardly any wind in his favor. Again in the present year Mr. H. M. Harriman came in first with a carry and roll of two hundred and forty yards under rather more favorable circumstances, because the ground was hard and level; but even so he had only a slight breeze behind him. These figures are absolutely correct, and yet they would be considered exceedingly high in Scotland. Driving is, of course, the easiest part of the game to the beginner; and yet it is consoling to know that in this respect, at least, we are not behind our friends in the old country.

THE RULES OF GOLF

AS REVISED BY
The Royal and Ancient Golf Club of St. Andrews
IN 1891

With Rulings and Interpretations by the Executive
Committee of the United States Golf Association in
1897

Preface

At a meeting of the executive committee of the United States Golf Association, held at the Shinnecock Hills Golf Club at South-ampton, Long Island, July 18, 1896, it was voted:

"That Mr. C. B. Macdonald and Mr. Laurence Curtis is appointed a special committee to interpret the rules of golf and to present their report for action at the annual meeting."

Owing to the unexpected amount of labor and investigation required, the committees were unable to make their report until June10, 1897, when the following codification of rules and rulings was duly presented to the executive committee and by them ratified and ordered to be promulgated and published as the law of the United States Golf Association.

The special committee have made no change in the words of the rules as they stand in the code of the Royal and Ancient Golf Club of St. Andrews, revised in 1891; but they have appended to said rules the rulings of the United States Golf Association, based upon the results of many decisions of committees or experts, or upon customs which have obtained in the best clubs in Scotland and England.

They hereby acknowledge with thanks, assistance and advice received from the following authorities: The editor of "Golf," and Messrs. Horace G. Hutchinson, Harold H. Hilton, Leslie Balfour Melville, W. T. Linskill, H. J. Whigham and others.

There will doubtless be found many points not covered in this work. Such are mostly those which should be made the subjects of local rules, or such as may be considered to belong to the etiquette of golf. Such would be questions as to: Dropping a ball at the edge of a hazard where it is impracticable to drop it behind the hazard.

(Rule 19 and Medal Rule 8.) Outsiders looking for a lost ball. (Rule 37.) Unplayable balls (Rule 38) or mud adhering to a ball.

Discontinuing play on account of sudden severe storms, or for taking refreshments.(Rule 11, Medal Play.) Lifting balls lying on putting greens other than the one played to. Casual water through the fair green.

Boundaries, walls, fences, gates, rabbit holes, gopher holes, direction flag's, etc. Strict definition of hazards on the course. Liability of players to suffer the full penalty when their caddies commit a breach of any rule. Restraint upon single players practicing on the course. Right of parties with caddies to pass parties without caddies, or a single to pass a foursome. Slow or inexperienced players blocking the course. Stringent rules for keeping scores in competitions.

Charles Blair Macdonald. Laurence Curtis.

Rules

Rule 1:

The game of golf is played by two or more sides, each playing its own ball. A side may consist of one or more persons.

RULING OF THE U. S. G. A.

Two sides of single players constitute a match called a "Single." Two sides of two players each constitute a "Foursome," and the players on either side are called "Partners."

Rule 2:

The game consists in each side playing a ball from a tee into a hole by successive strokes, and the hole is won by the side holing its ball in the fewest strokes, except as otherwise provided for in the rules. If two sides hole out in the same number of strokes, the hole is halved.

RULING OF THE U. S. G. A.

"Match Play " is decided by the number of holes won. "Medal Play "is decided by the aggregate number of strokes.

Unless otherwise stated, a match shall consist of the play of the game over eighteen holes of the links. By agreement a match may consist of the play over any number of holes. In match play, the player plays against an "Opponent," and opponents have certain privileges and responsibilities defined by the rules.

In medal play and bogey competitions the players are all "competitors" and have special privileges (Medal Rules 5, 6, 7 and 8), and a distinct responsibility. (Medal Rule 4.) u Col. Bogey " is an imaginary opponent against whose arbitrary score each player plays by holes; otherwise bogey competitions are governed by medal play rules, except that the player loses a hole: When the ball is struck twice, or is stopped by the player, or his caddie, or clubs; When a ball is lost; When a ball is not played wherever it lies, except as provided for in Rules 17 and 21.

Rule 3:

The teeing ground shall be indicated by two marks placed in a line at right angles to the course, and the players shall not tee in front of, nor on either side of these marks, nor more than two club lengths behind them. A ball played from outside the limits of the teeing ground, as thus defined, may be recalled by the opposite side. The hole shall be four and one quarter inches in diameter and at least four inches deep.

The penalty for playing the ball outside the limits, as thus defined, shall be: In match play, the ball may be recalled by the opposite side (no stroke being counted for the misplay). In medal play, the ball must be recalled (no stroke being counted for the misplay) or the player shall be disqualified. The option of recalling a ball is in all cases forfeited unless exercised at once before another stroke has been played.

Rule 4:

The ball must be fairly struck at and not pushed, scraped nor spooned, under penalty of the loss of the hole. Any movement of the club which is intended to strike the ball is a stroke.

RULING OF THE U. S. G. A.

Penalty for breach of this rule: In Match Play, loss of the hole. In Medal Play, disqualification.

Rule 5:

The game commences by each side playing a ball from the first teeing ground. In a match with two or more on a side the partners shall strike off alternately from the tees, and shall strike alternately during the play of the hole. The players, who are to strike against each other, shall be named at starting and shall continue in the same order during the match.

The player, who shall play first on each side, shall be named by his own side. In case of failure to agree, it shall be settled by lot or toss which side shall have the option of leading.

Rule 6:

If a player shall play when his partner should have done so, his side shall lose the hole, except in the case of the tee shot, when the stroke may be recalled at the option of the opponents.

Penalty for breach of this rule: In Match Play, loss of the hole. In Medal Play, if the player play the tee shot when his partner should have done so, the ball must be recalled (no stroke being counted for the misplay) or the side shall be disqualified. If a player play when his partner should have done so through the green, the ball shall be recalled and dropped, and a stroke counted for the misplay.

Rule 7:

The side winning a hole shall lead in starting for the next hole, and may recall the opponent's stroke should he plays out of order. This privilege is called the u honor. "On starting for a new match the winner of the long match in the previous round is entitled to the honor. Should the first match have been halved, the winner of the last hole gained is entitled to the honor.

In Match Play, the stroke recalled is not counted. In Medal Play, the stroke may not be recalled.

Rule 8:

One round of the links, generally eighteen holes, is a match, unless otherwise agreed upon. The match is won by the side which gets more holes ahead than there remain holes to be played, or by the side winning the last hole when the match was all even at the second last hole. If both sides have won the same number, it is a halved match.

In competitions: In Match Play, when two competitors have halved their match, they shall continue playing hole by hole till one or the other shall have won a hole, which shall determine the winner of the match. Should the match play competition be a handicap, the competitors must decide the tie by playing either one hole, three or five more holes, according to the manner in which the handicap ceded falls upon certain holes so as to make the game a fairly proportionate representation of the round.

In Medal Play, where two or more competitors are tied, the winner shall be determined by another round of the course; except that By Laws 15 and 19 of the United States Golf Association provide that, in case of ties for the sixteenth place in the Amateur Championship medal rounds, or the eighth place in the Women's Championship medal rounds, respectively, the contestants so tied shall continue to play until one or the other shall have gained a lead by strokes, the hole or holes to be played out.

Rule 9:

After the balls are struck from the tee, the ball furthest from the hole to which the parties are playing shall be played first, except as otherwise provided for in the Rules. Should the wrong side play first, the opponent may recall the stroke before his side has played.

In Match Play, no stroke is counted for the misplay if recalled. In Medal Play, the stroke may not be recalled.

Rule 10:

Unless with the opponent's consent, a ball struck from the tee shall not be changed, touched nor moved, before the hole is played out, under the penalty of one stroke, except as otherwise provided for in the Rules.

Penalty for breach of this rule: In Match Play, loss of one stroke. In Medal Play, loss of one stroke.

Rule 11:

In playing through the green all loose impediments within a club length of a ball, which is not lying in or touching a hazard, may be removed; but loose impediments which are more than a club length from the ball shall not be removed under penalty of one stroke.

Penalty for breach of this rule: In Match Play, loss of one stroke. In Medal Play, loss of one stroke. Ice, snow and hail within a club length of the ball through the green may be removed; but on the putting green the ice, snow and hail may only be removed as per Rule 34, "by brushing lightly with the hand only across the put, and not along it."

Rule 12:

Before striking at the ball the player shall not move, bend nor break anything fixed or growing near the ball, except in the act of placing his feet on the ground for the purpose of addressing the ball, and in soling his club to address the ball, under the penalty of the loss of the hole, except as provided for in Rule 18.

Penalty for breach of this rule: In Match Play, loss of the hole. In Medal Play, disqualification.

Rule 13:

A ball stuck fast in wet ground or sand may be taken out and replaced loosely in the hole which it has made.

Rule 14:

When a ball lies in or touches a hazard, the club shall not touch the ground, nor shall anything be touched or moved before the player strikes at the ball, except that the player may place his feet firmly on the ground for the purpose of addressing the ball, under the penalty of the loss of the hole. But if in the backward or in the downward swing any grass, bent, whin or other growing substance, or the side of a bunker or wall, paling or other immovable obstacle, be touched, no penalty shall be incurred.

Penalty for breach of this rule: In Match Play, loss of the hole. In Medal Play, for moving anything, disqualification; for touching anything, loss of one stroke. The intent of this ruling is to prevent the player from altering or improving the lie of the ball. The club shall not be soled, nor the surface of the ground be touched within a radius of a club length from the ball, except that the player may place his feet firmly on the ground for the purpose of addressing the ball; but nothing herein shall be construed as allowing a player to test in any manner the consistency of the sand or soil in any part of the hazard, under penalty of disqualification.

When a ball lies on turf in a hazard or surrounded by a hazard, it shall be considered as being on the fair green, e., and the club may be soled.

Rule 15:

A " hazard " shall be any bunker of whatever nature water, sand, loose earth, mole hills, paths, roads of railways, whins, bushes, rushes, rabbit scrapes, fences, ditches, or anything which is not the ordinary green of the course, except sand blown on to the grass by wind or sprinkled on the grass for the preservation of the links, or snow or ice or bare patches on the course.

Long grass or casual water on the fair green are not hazards. Woods are hazards. The fair green shall be considered any part of a course except the hazards and putting greens.

Rule 16:

A player, or a player's caddie, shall not press down nor remove any irregularities of surface near the ball, except at the teeing ground, under the penalty of the loss of the hole. Penalty for breach of this rule: In Match Play, loss of the hole. In Medal Play, disqualification. "Near the ball " shall be considered within a club length. Pressing down the surface near the ball by prolonged or forcible soling of the club shall be deemed a breach of this rule.

Rule 17:

If any vessel, wheelbarrow, tool, roller, grass cutter, box or other similar obstruction has been placed upon the course, such obstruction may be removed. A ball lying on or touching such obstruction, or on clothes or nets, or on ground under repair or temporarily covered up or opened, may be lifted and dropped at the nearest point of the course; but a ball lifted in a hazard shall be dropped in a hazard. A ball lying in a golf hole or flag hole may be lifted and dropped not more than a club length behind such hole.

Rule 18:

When a ball is completely covered with fog , bent, whins, etc., only so much thereof shall be set aside as that the player may have a view of his ball before he plays, whether in a line with the hole or otherwise.

RULING OF THE U. S. G. A.

Penalty for breach of this rule: In Match Play, loss of the hole. In Medal Play, disqualification. The "etc." in this rule includes grass, bushes, plants, hedges, trees and foliage.

Rule 19:

When a ball is to be dropped the player shall drop it. He shall front the hole, stand erect behind the hazard, keep the spot from which the ball was lifted, or, in the case of running water, the spot at which it entered, in a line between him and the hole, and drop the ball behind him from his head, standing as far behind the hazard as he may please.

Penalty for breach of this rule: In Match Play, if the ball has not been dropped in strict accordance with the rule, the opponent has the option of having the ball dropped again. In Medal Play, if the ball has not been dropped in strict accordance with the rule, the other competitor must call for the ball to be dropped again, and the player must comply or be disqualified. The player must drop the ball himself, not his caddie nor his partner. A dropped ball shall not be considered in play until at rest.

When a ball is lifted from a hazard and dropped and falls back into the hazard, the player may lift again without further penalty.

Rule 20:

When the balls in play lie within six inches of each other, measured from their nearest points, the ball nearer the hole shall be lifted until the other is played, and shall then be replaced as nearly as possible in its original position.

Should the ball further from the hole be accidentally moved in so doing, it shall be replaced. Should the lie of the lifted ball be altered by the opponent in playing", it may be replaced in a lie near to, and as nearly as possible similar to, that from which it was lifted.

Rule 21:

If the ball lie or be lost in water, the player may drop a ball under the penalty of one stroke.

RULING OF THE U. S. G. A.

When the ball lies in casual water on the putting green, it may be lifted without penalty and replaced by hand to one side but not nearer to the hole. A ball in water in a hazard may be lifted and dropped behind the water or hazard, under penalty of one stroke.

Rule 22:

Whatever happens by accident to a ball in motion: such as its being deflected or stopped by any agency outside of the match, or by the forecaddie, is a "rub of the green," and the ball shall be played from where it lies. Should a ball lodge in anything moving, such ball, or, if it cannot be recovered, another ball shall be dropped as nearly as possible at the spot where the object was when the ball lodged in it.

But if a ball at rest be displaced by any agency outside the match, the player shall drop it, or another ball, as nearly as possible at the spot where it lay. On the putting green the ball may be replaced by hand. Penalty for breach of this rule: In Match Play, loss of the hole. In Medal Play, disqualification. Wind and weather are not agencies "outside the match."

Rule 23:

If the player's ball strike, or be accidentally moved by, an opponent or an opponent's caddie or clubs, the opponent loses the hole. Penalty incurred: In Match Play, loss of the hole.

In Medal Play, no penalty. If the player's ball strikes the other competitor or his caddie or clubs, it is a "rub of the green," and the ball shall be played from where it lies. If the player's ball at rest be accidentally or intentionally moved by the other competitor or his caddie, the ball must be replaced.

Rule 24:

If the player's ball strike or be stopped by himself or his partner or either of their caddies or clubs, or if, while in the act of playing, the player shall strike the ball twice, his side loses the hole.

Penalty for breach of this rule: In Match Play, loss of the hole. In Medal Play, loss of one stroke.

Rule 25:

If the player, when not making a stroke, or his partner or either of their caddies, touches their side's ball, except at the tee, so as to move it, or by touching anything cause it to move, the penalty is one stroke.

Penalty incurred: In Match Play, loss of one stroke. In Medal Play, loss of one stroke. Except at the tee, if the ball moves while the player is addressing it, the player loses one stroke. Except at the tee, if the ball be struck while moving, the penalty is one stroke, u e., one stroke for the moving and one stroke for the play. Except at the tee, if struck at while moving and missed, one stroke shall be counted for the moving and another for the miss.

Rule 26:

A ball is considered to have been moved if it leaves its original position in the least degree and stop in another; but if a player touches his ball and thereby causes it to oscillate, without causing it to leave its original position; it is not moved in the sense of Rule 25.

Rule 27:

A player's side loses a stroke if he play the opponent's ball, unless: (1) the opponent then play the player's ball, whereby the penalty is canceled, and the hole must be played out with the balls thus exchanged; or (2) the mistake occur through wrong information given by the opponent, in which case the mistake, if discovered before the opponent has played, must be rectified by placing a ball as nearly as possible where the opponent's ball lay.

If it be discovered before either side has struck off at the tee that one side has played out the previous hole with the ball of a party not engaged in the match, that side loses the hole.

RULING OF THE U. S. G. A.

Penalty for breach of this rule: 1st. Playing the opponent's ball with exceptions (1) and (2) above noted. In the Rule: In Match Play, loss of one stroke. The ball must be replaced. In Medal Play, no penalty. The ball must be replaced. 2d. Playing out with the ball of a party not engaged in the match:

In Match Play, if discovered before the next tee stroke, loss of the hole. In Medal Play, the player must go back and play his own ball, or, not finding it, return as nearly as possible to the spot where it was last struck, tee another ball and lose a stroke (Rule 5, Medal Play), or else be disqualified.

Rule 28:

If a ball be lost, the player's side loses the hole. A ball shall be considered as lost if it be not found within five minutes after the search is begun.

RULING OF THE U. S. G. A.

Penalty incurred: In Match Play, loss of the hole. Where both balls are lost at the same time, neither side wins the hole, which should be called halved, irrespective of the number of strokes that either side may have played. A player who has lost his ball may, before giving up the hole, ask the opponent to show his (the opponent's) ball. In Medal Play, loss of one stroke and distance. The player must return as nearly as possible to the spot where the ball was struck, tee another ball and lose one stroke. But if the ball be found before he has struck the other ball, the first ball shall continue in play.

Rule 29:

A ball must be played wherever it lies, or the hole given up, except as otherwise provided for in the Rules.

RULING OF THE U. S. G. A.

Penalty: In Match Play, loss of the hole. In Medal Play, loss of two strokes and ball may be teed. The exceptions are provided for in Rules 17 and 21.

Rule 30:

The term "putting green" shall mean the ground within twenty yards of the hole, excepting hazards.

RULING OF THE U. S. G. A.

If a hazard be within the twenty yard limit of the hole, the ground outside of such hazard may not be considered as putting green, even though it is within the twenty yard radius from the hole.

Rule 31:

All loose impediments may be removed from the putting green, except the opponent's ball, when at a greater distance from the player's than six inches.

In Medal Play, on the putting green, the ball nearer the hole may be holed out or lifted at its owner's option if "it be in such a position that it might, if left, give an advantage to the other competitor."(Rule 9, Medal Play.)

Rule 32:

In a match of three or more sides a ball in any degree lying between the player and the hole must be lifted, or, if on the putting green, holed out.

Rule 33:

When the ball is on the putting green, no mark shall be placed nor line drawn as a guide; the line to the hole may be pointed out, but the person doing so may not touch the ground with the hand or club. The player may have his own or his partner's caddie to stand at the hole, but none of the players, nor their caddies, may move so as to shield the ball from, or expose it to, the wind. The penalty for any breach of this rule is the loss of the hole.

Penalty for breach of this rule: In Match Play, loss of the hole. In Medal Play, disqualification. The putting line shall not be considered to extend beyond the hole.

Rule 34:

The player or his caddie may remove(but not press down) sand, earth, worm casts or snow lying around the hole or on the line of his put. This shall be done by brushing lightly with the hand only across the put, and not along it. Dung may be removed to a side by an iron club, but the club must not be laid with more than its own weight upon the ground. The putting line must not be touched by club, hand or foot, except as above authorized, or immediately in front of the ball in the act of addressing it, under the penalty of the loss of the hole.

RULING OF THE U. S. G. A.

Penalty for breach of this rule: In Match Play, loss of the hole. In Medal Play, disqualification. The putting line shall not be considered to extend beyond the hole. The "player or his caddie " shall include his partner and his partner's caddie.

Rule 35:

Either side is entitled to have the flag stick removed when approaching the hole. If a ball rest against the flag stick when in the hole, the player shall be entitled to remove the stick, and, if the ball fall in, it shall be considered as holed out in the previous stroke.

Penalty for putting at the hole with the flag stick in it and striking the flag stick: In Match Play, no penalty .In Medal Play, disqualification.

Rule 36:

A player shall not play until the opponent's ball shall have ceased to roll, under the penalty of one stroke. Should the player's ball knock in the opponent's ball, the latter shall be counted as holed out in the previous stroke. If, in playing, the player's ball displaces the opponent's ball, the opponent shall have the option of replacing it.

Penalty under this rule; In Match Play, loss of one stroke. In Medal Play, loss of one stroke. Should the player's ball knock in the opponent's ball: In Match Play, the latter shall be counted as holed out in the previous stroke? In Medal Play, the latter must be replaced. Should the player's ball displace the opponent's ball: In Match Play, the latter shall have the option of replacing his ball, and must exercise such option at once and before any further play? In Medal Play, the latter must replace his ball.

A player having holed out his ball in the like or the odd may knock away the opponent's ball from the lip of the hole and claim the hole if he had holed in the like or a half if he had holed in the odd.

Rule 37:

A player shall not ask for advice, nor be knowingly advised, about the game by word, look or gesture from anyone except his own caddie or his partner or partner's caddie, under the penalty of the loss of the hole.

RULING OF THE U. S. G. A.

Penalty for breach of this rule; In Match Play, loss of the hole. In Medal Play, disqualification.

Rule 38:

If a ball split into separate pieces, another ball may be put down where the largest portion lies; or if two pieces are apparently of equal size, it may be put where either piece lies, at the option of the player. If a ball crack, or become unplayable, the player may change it on intimating to his opponent his intention to do so.

Rule 39:

A penalty stroke shall not be counted the stroke of a player, and shall not affect the rotation of the play.

A "stroke" is any movement of the club which is intended to strike the ball. A player who while addressing his ball intentionally or accidentally causes it to move, shall be considered to have played one stroke (except at the tee). A "penalty stroke" is a stroke added to the score of a side for infringing certain rules.

Rule 40:

Should a dispute arise on any point, the players have the right of determining the party or parties to whom the dispute shall be referred; but should they not agree, either party may refer it to the Green Committee of the green where the dispute occurs, and their decision shall be final. Should the dispute not be covered by the Rules of Golf, the arbiters must decide it by equity.

Such decisions may be finally referred to the Executive Committee of the United States Golf Association.

Special Rules for Medal Play

Rule 1:

In club competitions the competitor doing the stipulated course in fewest strokes shall be the winner.

Rule 2:

If the lowest score be made by two or more competitors, the ties shall be decided by another round to be played either on the same day or on any other day, as the Captain, or in his absence the Secretary, shall direct.

RULING OF THE U. S. G. A.

Except that By laws 15 and 19 of the United States Golf Association provide that, in case of ties for the sixteenth place in the amateur championship medal rounds, or for the eighth place in the women's championship medal rounds, respectively, the contestants so tied shall continue to play until one or the other shall have gained a lead by strokes, the hole or holes to be played out.

Rule 3:

New holes shall be made for the medal round, and thereafter no member shall play any stroke on the putting green before competing.

Penalty for breach of this rule is disqualification. Competitors must always assume that new holes have been made, whether really made or not. Trial strokes may be played through the fair green, but no stroke may be played within twenty yards of any hole on the course where the competition takes place. In match play competitions, other than bogey competitions, a member may play upon the putting greens.

Rule 4:

The scores shall be kept by a special marker, or by the competitors noting each other's scores. The scores marked shall be checked at the finish of each hole. On the completion of the course the score of the player shall be signed by the person keeping the score and handed to the Secretary.

Penalty for breach of this rule is disqualification. The score must be handed to the Secretary or to some person designated by the green Committee. A caddie may not keep score, nor may an outsider (a player not in competition) playing with a competitor do so without the sanction of the club's executive. It is commended, but not required, to mark down each stroke as played.

Rule 5:

If a ball be lost, the player shall return as nearly as possible to the spot where the ball was struck, tee another ball and lose a stroke. If the lost ball be found before he has struck the other ball, the first shall continue in play.

RULING OF THE U. S. G. A.

Penalty for breach of this rule is disqualification.

Rule 6:

If the player's ball strike himself or his clubs or caddie, or if in the act of playing the player strike the ball twice, the penalty shall be one stroke.

RULING OF THE U. S. G. A.

If the player's ball strikes a forecaddie, it is a "rub of the green."

Rule 7:

If a competitor's ball strikes the other player or his club or caddie, it is a "rub of the green," and the ball shall be played from where it lies.

Rule 8:

A ball may, under a penalty of two strokes, be lifted out of a difficulty of any description, and be teed behind the same.

Rule 9:

All balls shall be holed out, and when play is on the putting green the flag shall be removed, and the competitor whose ball is nearest to the hole shall have the option of holing out first, or of lifting his ball, if it be in such a position that it might, if left, give an advantage to the other competitor. Throughout the green a competitor can have the other competitor's ball lifted, if he fined that it interferes with his stroke.

RULING OF THE U. S. G. A.

Penalty for breach of this rule is disqualification. Either player may judge whether the balls as they lie give the other an advantage. If a ball at rest be caused by any agency outside the match to roll into the hole, the ball shall not be considered as holed out in the previous stroke, but shall be replaced as nearly as possible in the same position as occupied before it was displaced. Should a competitor hole out with a ball other than his own, he shall be disqualified, unless he can g o back and resume play with his original ball, or, failing to find it return as nearly as possible to the spot where it was last struck, tee another ball and lose a stroke. (Rule 5, Medal Play.)

Rule 10:

A competitor may not play with a professional, and he may not receive advice from anyone but his caddie. A forecaddie may be employed.

RULING OF THE U. S. G. A.

Penalty for breach of this rule is disqualification. Each competitor may have a forecaddie.

Rule 11:

Competitors may not discontinue play because of bad weather.

RULING OF THE U. S. G. A.

Penalty for breach of this rule is disqualification.

Rule 12:

The penalty for a breach of any rule shall be disqualification.

Rule 13:

Any dispute regarding the play shall be determined by the Green Committee.

Rule 14:

The ordinary rules of golf, so far as they are not at variance with the special rules, shall apply to medal play.

*Note: All up-to-date rules can be found on ww.usga.org/playing/rules/rules.html

Etiquette of Golf

1. No player, caddie or on looker should move or talk during a stroke.

2. No player should play from the tee until the party in front has played their second strokes and are out of range, nor play to the putting green till the party in front have holed out and moved away.

3. The player who leads from the tee should be allowed to play before his opponent tees his ball.

4. Players who have holed out should not try their puts over again when other players are following them.

5. Players looking for a lost ball must allow any other match coming up to pass them.

6. A party playing three or more balls must allow a two ball match to pass them.

7. A party playing a shorter round must allow a two ball match playing the whole round to pass them.

8. A player should not put at the hole when the flag is in it.

9. The reckoning of the strokes is kept by the terms "the odd," "two more,""three more," etc., and "one off three,""one of two," "the like." The reckoning of the holes is kept by the terms so many "holes up" or "all even" and so many "to play."

10. Turf cut or displaced by a stroke in playing should be at once replaced.

Choosing Clubs in 2011

At the time this book was written the game was played with basically the same set of clubs that we took the time to cover in this book. The standard set includes 3 woods (1, 3, and 5 wood), 10 irons (2 to 9 iron, PW, SW), and a putter. It's time to take a look at some of the technological advancements in clubs and how can you take advantage of new improvements to improve your game. This section will give both beginners and advanced golfers a look at the best way to choose a club.

Sometimes a shot requires distance and sometimes it requires accuracy. Some shots we hit from a tee, some we play from short grass and sometimes even from oh-so-dreaded places like rough, sand and dry dirt (hardpan). Each of such situations will benefits from a different club you use. Based on our abilities, some shots will be relatively easy and some will be a pain in neck.

If the challenge you face is a 200 yard carry over water to a rather tight pin on a small green, the proper choice of club for a beginner, intermediate or advanced golfer will be different. In the past all three were left with only a few club choices, but - thankfully - today there are many more.

By far the most frequent shot is a putt. For an average golfer, the putter is used more than twice as much as any other club. Statistically, if a golfer shoots a score of 100, 35% - 40% of those strokes will be putts. So, quite obviously, the putter is the most important club you carry.

Generally, for most golfers the driver (also called the #1 wood) is used the next most often, about 14 times from the tee, or roughly 12-20% of the time depending on ability level and course requirements. A good drive makes the rest of the shots on that hole easier. That makes the driver a very important club.

For players who have a hard time hitting the green in a regulation number of strokes, the wedges may be the second most used category of clubs. Even on a good day a beginner may spend a 15 to 20 strokes chipping up to the green.

The remaining challenges in a round will utilize the rest of the clubs in your set. It is likely that no one club will be used more than a few times. This means, in terms of club usage, the putter, driver and wedges are clearly used the most frequently while the rest of the clubs will bring up the rear.

In addition, a club that is tough to hit must be given added weight. The more difficult it is to hit a particular club the more likely it is to cause disaster. The driver, the long irons, and fairway woods are the most likely culprits to cause that terrible shot.

As a Beginner you probably have a hard time making consistent contact with the ball. Hitting it with the heel and toe of the club, topping the ball or hitting the ground first (fat shots) will be your challenge. As beginner you may also have trouble getting the clubhead to the ball in a square position. This means your clubhead generally approaches the ball from outside of the target line (out-to-in) and at a steep angle. This results in your typical shot shape being a slice - a shot that curves right. [For additional insights on how to cure a slice you may want to consult David Nevogt's eBook on *The Perfect Golf Swing*.]

In short, you have a problem hitting the ball with the center of the clubface. Your swing speed is slow due to lack of experience with proper swing mechanics. Generally, for women and juniors, clubhead speed is slow due to lack of strength, causing difficulty in getting the ball up in the air, and a lack of distance.

The ideal set for a beginner would be one that takes into account the swing/hit issues mentioned above. Maximum forgiveness is the goal.

To help with inconsistent contact an oversized clubhead will help. An oversized club has a larger hitting area so there will be fewer missed hits. For irons, perimeter weighting will help to make those missed hits go a little straighter. You're shots off the heel and toe will be more solid. A wide sole will slide through the turf easier and get the ball up higher.

Slightly shorter clubs will make accurate club-to-ball contact a higher possibility.

To help with that out-to-in swing path, an offset clubhead will get the clubface back to the ball a little later. That means the clubface will be more square to the target and not open. This will also keep the hands a little bit in front of the clubhead, which in turn will also help with those fat shots. A clubhead with adjustable weights can help to adapt the club to your particular swing pattern.

For long shots from the fairway or rough a beginner should choose woods and hybrid clubs with the most loft possible, together with a low center of gravity. More loft means it will be easier to get the ball in the air, and it will likely go a little farther as well. In addition it will create more backspin which will counteract the side spin of shots and keep them from curving as much. As a combined result your shots will be a little bit straighter.

A beginner's driver should have a larger head (over 430cc) to increase the size of the hitting area. Additional loft (12-15 degrees) will get the ball in the air. Added loft once again will increase backspin and make those left to right curves less of a head ache.

Putting is something that, with practice, will get better (although sometimes hard to believe). It's true, it doesn't take great athletic ability to be a decent putter. Yet again, it's still hard for a beginner to judge distances so 3 putts are still common. Besides keeping your head directly over the ball a good alignment system will also help getting over your inconsistency.

Super Game Improvement (SGI) irons are the choice for maximum forgiveness. SGI clubs will offer maximum perimeter weighting, larger offset, a wide sole, and low center of gravity. Club choices can be 6 iron through pitching wedge or 6-sand wedge. The sand wedge selection should offer extra "bounce". Bounce is the feature on the sole of the club that helps it easily glide through sand or rough.

While you are allowed to carry 14 clubs you actually don't need them. The first clubs to leave out are the long irons (3, 4). Your iron set should start with the 5 or 6 iron and go up to the sand wedge (SW). For longer shots use lofted woods (5, 7, 9) and hybrid clubs (3, 4, 5). You may find you still hit them all about the same distance, so if you can experiment, test them all to see which ones feel the best. Don't take the ones that you don't hit well and leave them at home. You should still buy them because you will get better and need them later.

The right set also depends on swing speed. Swing speeds between 65-80 mph (women, juniors and some seniors) will need more woods and hybrid clubs and generally more loft to help get the ball up in the air. Average male swing speeds of 80-90 mph can begin to add a few more irons (5-6), but you still want to use hybrids and lofted woods instead of long irons. Woods are always easier to hit for beginners.

Their larger heads and flat soles compared to irons create more confidence. Slightly shortened versions of 3, 5, and 7 woods (-.5") are highly recommended for all beginners regardless of swing speed.

The driver should have a 440-460 cc titanium head. The new large headed drivers are easier to hit, no second thoughts about it. Make sure you have extra loft to increase accuracy and distance. If you find you still have problems hitting it accurately, try choking up an inch or so.

For a putter, you want one of the new large headed mallet putters. These new putters have greater MOI (they don't twist on mishits) and their alignment aids make short putts much easier.

Your set configuration should be: Woods (1, 3), Hybrids (3, 4, 5), Irons (Super Game Improvement) (6-SW), Putter (Mallet)

---

* A wedge is an iron used for short shots that has a high-loft - pitching wedge, sand wedge.

The Golf Dictionary

A

Ace - A hole made in one stroke

Address - The stance taken by a player in preparing to hit the ball. The positioning of your body in relationship to the golf ball. Same as "addressing the ball".

Albatross - Scoring three under par is generally referred to as "Albatross". It follows the 'bird' theme for shots below par: birdie for one under par and eagle for two under (see below).

Amateur - A golfer who plays without monetary compensation.

Angle of approach - The angle or degree at which the club moves downward, or upward, toward the ball.

Approach shot - Normally a short or medium shot played to the putting green or pin.

Apron - The grassy area surrounding the putting surface. See fringe.

Attend the flag - To hold and then remove the flag while another player putts.

Away - The ball that is the greatest distance from the hole when more than one golfer is playing. It is the first to be played.

B

Back nine - The last 9 holes of an 18 hole course.

Backspin - A reverse spin placed on the ball to make in stop short on the putting surface.

Backswing - The backward part of the swing starting from the ground and going back over the head.

Balata - A hard, resilient sap-like substance from the South American Balata tree that is used to make a cover for rubber-cored golf balls.

Ball - The round object which we attempt to hit into the hole. Prior to the 17th century it was made of wood or wool in a leather cover. After the 17th century feathers were boiled and compressed, then sewn in a leather cover. It continued to evolve to a solid gutta percha (or a mixture with gutta percha other substances) in the 1850's and strip rubber wound around a core in the 1900's. Presently made of solid compressed synthetic rubber with hundreds of surface indentations which aid in the flight of the ball.

Ball marker - A token or a small coin used to spot the balls position on the green.

Ball retriever - A long pole with a scoop on the end which is used to collect balls from water hazards and other areas.

Ball washer - A device for cleaning golf balls.

Bend - The curve on a shot created by sidespin.

Bent grass - Type of grass seen for the most part on Northern courses. It is of the genus Agrostis, native to North America and Eurasia. It is a hardy and resilient type of grass that can be cut very short.

Bermuda - Type of grass seen mostly on Southern courses in North America. Of the type Cynodon dactylon. Originally native to southern Europe. It was introduced to warmer areas of the world to be used on courses where bent grass will not grow.

Best ball - A match in which one player plays against the better of two balls or the best ball of three players. Also the better score of two partners in a four-ball or best-ball match.

Birdie - One stroke under par for a hole. Also possibly derived from the term "It flew like a bird" to indicate a good shot.

Bite - The backspin imparted on the ball that makes the ball stop dead, or almost so, with little or no roll.

Blade - A. The hitting part of an iron clubhead, not including the hosel. B. To hit the ball with the leading edge of the blade of an iron.

Blade Putter - A type of putter with an iron head with the basic form the same as other standard numbered irons.

Blast - A shot that takes a large amount of sand with it when hitting out of a sand trap. An explosion shot.

Block - To play a shot by delaying the rotation of the wrists during a swing. This causes the clubface not to be square at the point of impact resulting in a sliced ball.

Bogey - A score of one over par for the hole. To play a hole in one stroke over par.

Boundary - The edge of the golf course that defines the area of play, spectator, etc. and bounces back into play. Sample usage: "I would have bogeyed the fourth.

Bunker - A depression in bare ground that is usually covered with sand. Also called a "sand trap". It is considered a hazard under the Rules of Golf.

Burn - The Scottish term for a creek or stream

C

Caddie (caddy) - Someone who carries a player's club during play and offers him assistance in accordance with the rules.

Card - A card used to record scores in stroke play.

Cart - A two-wheeled trolley on which a golf is fitted and pulled around the course.

Casual - water Any temporary accumulations of water that are visible before or after a player takes his stance and is not a hazard or in a water hazard. A player may lift his ball from casual water without penalty.

Center shafted - Putter in which the shaft is joined to the center of the head.

Chip shot - A short approach shot of low trajectory usually hit from near the green. It is normally hit with overspin or bite.

Chip-and-run - A chip shot including the run of the ball after landing.

Choke - To grip down farther on the club handle.

Closed stance - The left foot extends over the balls line of flight while the right foot is back

Closed face - When the clubface is pointed to the left of the target when you address the ball.

Closed stance - A stance taken with the right foot pulled back, away from the ball.

Club - The implement used in golf to strike the ball. Consists of a shaft, grip and a clubhead of wood or metal.

Club head - The hitting area of the club.

Clubhouse - The main building on the course. collar The grassy fringe surrounding the putting green.

Compression - The flattening of the ball against the clubface at impact. Also the degree of resilience of a ball.

Core - The center of the golf ball.

Course - The playing area which is usually made up of 9 or 18 holes with each hole having a tee off area, fairway and green.

Course rating - The comparison of playing one course as opposed to another in terms of difficulty. It is expressed in strokes or decimal fractions of strokes. The yardage of the course and the ability of a scratch golfer are the basis for determination.

Cross-handed grip - A grip where your left hand is below the right.

Cup - The container in the hole holds the flagstick in pace.

Cut shot - A controlled shot that results in the ball stopping almost immediately on the green without roll.

D

Dimple - The round indentations on the golf ball cover which are scientifically designed to enable the ball to make a steady and true flight.

Divot - A piece of turf removed with by the club when making a shot. It is always replaced and tamped down.

Dogleg - A left or right bend in the fairway

Dormie - When playing in match play, being five up with five to go, four up with four left, etc. To be as many holes up as there are to play.

Double bogey - A score of two over par for a single hole.

Double eagle - A score of three under par for a single hole.

Downhill lie - When addressing the ball and your right foot is higher than your left (for right-handed players).

Downswing - The motion of swinging a club from the top of the swing to the point of impact.

Draw shot - A controlled "hook" used to get in position for the next shot or get out of trouble. A shot that curves from left to right. To play a shot so that it curves owing to sidespin from right to left with a right-handed player. Conversely from right to left for a left-handed player.

Drive - To hit the ball with maximum force and full stroke. Usually with a driver from the tee.

Drive-and-pitch - The type of hole on which the green can be reached with a drive and a pitch. Could also refer to a course where all holes are of this type.

Driver - The longest-hitting modern wooden club, used primarily from the tee when maximum distance is required. Also called the No. 1 wood. driving range An area or building used for the purpose of practicing tee-shots and other strokes.

Drop - To deposit the ball on the course after which you put the ball back in play after it has been declared unplayable or after the ball has been lost.

E

Eagle - Two strokes under par for a single hole. To play a hole at 2 under par.

Eight-iron - An iron club giving distance of between 115-150 yards. Also called a pitching niblick.

Equipment - Anything that is used by a player or is carried or worn. His ball in play is not included.

Explode - To hit the ball from sand using a steeply lofted club with the club hitting into the sand behind the ball and spraying a large amount of sand.

Explosion shot - A shot that takes large quantities of sand out of a sand trap.

Extra hole - As with extra innings, golfers play extra hole to break a tie.

F

Face - The hitting area or surface of the club head.

Fade - A term used to describe the slight turning of the ball from left to right (by a right-handed player) at the end of its flight. From right to left for a left-handed player.

Fairway - The area of the course between the tee and the green that is well-maintained allowing a good lie for the ball

Fairway wood - Any other wooden club other than a driver.

Featherie - An old leather ball stuffed with compressed feathers. Replaced by the gutta percha after 1848. Also spelled feathery.

Fescue - Grass of the genus Festuca, widely used on for rough on golf courses.

Five-iron - An iron club used for distances between 145-180 yards for men's clubs. Also known as a mashie.

Five-wood - A wooden club used for distances between 190-210 yards for men's clubs.

Flag - The marker attached to the flagstick.

Flagstick - A movable marker to show the location of the hole.

Flange - The additional surface of the club head which protrudes at the sole.

Flex - The amount of bend or the degree of stiffness of the club shaft.

Follow-through - The continuation of the swing after the ball has been hit.

Fore - An expression used to warn anyone who may be in danger from the flight of the ball. forecaddie Someone employed by the course or tournament committee to mark the position of a player's ball

Foursome - A term given to four players playing together. Also a match in which two players play against another two players with each side playing one ball.

Free drop - A drop where no penalty stroke is incurred.

Fringe - Same as "apron"

Front side - The first nine holes of an 18 hole course.

G

Gallery - The group of tournament spectators.

Gimme - A putt that is certain to be made on the next shot and will most likely be conceded by an opponent.

Golf glove - A glove generally worn by a right-handed golfer on the left hand, and by a left-handed golfer on the right hand, to improve the grip.

Goose-neck - Having the neck of a club curved so that the heel is slightly offset from the line of the shaft.

Grain - The direction in which the grass on a putting lies after it has been shortly cut

Graphite - A lightweight material used to make shafts and clubheads.

Green- The whole golf course according to golf rules. However, in popular usage, it refers to the putting surface.

Green fee - The charge made by the course to allow the player to use the course.

Greenkeeper - The employee of the club who is responsible for the maintenance of the course.

Greenside - Adjacent to the putting green.

Grip - The part of the shaft by which the club is held. Covered with leather or other material. Also means the manner in which you hold the club.

Groove - Linear scoring on a clubface.

Gross - The total number of strokes required to complete a round of golf BEFORE the player's handicap is deducted.

Grounding the club - Placing the clubhead behind the ball at address.

Ground under repair - any part of the course so marked by order of the Committee or so declared by its authorized representative. It includes material piled for removal and a hole made by a greenkeeper, even if not so marked.
All ground and any grass, bush, tree or other growing thing within the ground under repair is part of the ground under repair. The margin of ground under repair extends vertically downward, but not upward. Stakes and lines defining ground under repair are in such ground. Such stakes are obstructions. A ball is in ground under repair when it lies in or any part of it touches the ground under repair.

Note: The Committee may make a Local Rule prohibiting play from ground under repair or an environmentally-sensitive area defined as ground under repair.

Gutta percha - Material used in the manufacture of early golf balls. It was a hard, molded substance made from the sap of several types of Malaysian trees. These balls were in use from 1848 until the early 1900's.

H

Halved - When a match is played without a decision. A hole is "halved" when both sides play it in the same number of strokes

Handicap - The number of strokes a player may deduct from his actual score to adjust his scoring ability to the level of a scratch golfer. It is designed to allow golfers of different abilities to basically compete on the same level.

Hazard - A hazard is any sand trap, bunker or water on the course that may cause difficulty.

Head - The part of the club that makes contact with the ball. Usually made of wood, iron or some substitute material.

Heel - The part of the club head nearest the shaft.

Hickory - Wood from a native North American tree used at the beginning of the 19th century to make club shafts. Use continued until the 1920's.

Hit - To play a shot or stroke.

Hole - A 4 1/2" round receptacle in the green - at least 4" deep. Also refers to one of the nine or eighteen areas between the tee and the green.

Hole in one - A hole made with one stroke. Same as "ace"

Hole out - To complete the play for one hole by hitting the ball into the cup

Honor - The privilege of hitting first from the tee. Usually assigned at the first tee. After the first tee, the privilege goes to the winner of the last hole.

Hook - To hit the ball in a manner that causes it to curve from right to left in the case of a right-handed player or left to right for a left hander.

Hosel - The hollow part of an iron club head into which the shaft is fitted

I

Impact - The moment when the ball strikes the club.

In - The second nine holes as opposed to out - the first nine holes.

In play - Within the course (not out of bounds).

Inside - Being nearer the hole than the ball of your opponent.

Interlocking grip - A type of grip where the little finger of the left hand is intertwined with the index finger of the right hand for a right handed player. The converse applies to a left hander.

Intended line - The line you expect the ball to travel after hit.

Iron - Any one of a number of clubs with a head made of iron or steel. See definitions for individual clubs "two iron" etc. jungle A slang term for heavy rough.

L

Lag - To putt the ball with the intention leaving it short to ensure being able to hole out on the next stroke

Lateral hazard - Any hazard running parallel to the line of play

Lie - The position in which the ball rests on the ground. The lie can be good or bad in terms of the nature of ground where is rests, the slope, and the level of difficulty in playing it. The number of strokes a player is to have played during the hole.

Line - The correct path of a putt to the hole when putting. Also when on the fairway, the correct direction in which the ball to be played toward the putting green.

Lip - The top rim of the hole or cup

Lob shot - A shot that goes straight up and comes almost straight down with very little spin or forward momentum. Useful when there is not much green to play to.

Local rules - A set of rules for a club determined by the members.

Loft - The elevation of the ball in the air. Also means the angle at which the club face is set from the vertical and is used to lift the ball into the air. It is measured precisely as the angle between the face and a line parallel to the shaft.

Long game - Shots hit with the woods and long irons.

Long irons - The relatively straight-face and longer hitting irons.

Loose impediments - Any natural object that is not fixed or growing. This can include loose stones, twigs, branches, molehills, dung, worms and insects

M

Mallet - A putter that has a head that is much wider and heavier than that of a blade putter.

Marker - A small object, like a coin, that is used to mark the spot of the ball when it is lifted off the putting green.

Markers - The objects placed at the teeing round that indicate the area in which players must tee their balls.

Marshal - A person appointed by a tournament committee to keep order and handle spectators.

Match play - A competition played with each hole being a separate contest. The team or player winning the most holes, rather than having the lowest score, is the winner. The winner of the first hole is "one up". Even if the player wins that hole by two or three strokes, he is still only "one up". The lead is increased every time the player wins another hole. The winner is the one who wins the most holes. This was the original form of golf competition.

Meadowland - A lush grassland course.

Municipal course - A public course owned by local government.

N-O

Nine - A nine hole course or the sequence of 9 holes of an 18 hole course.

Obstruction - Any artificial object that has been left or placed on the course with the exception of course boundary markers and constructed roads and paths.

Off-centre - A poor hit.

Offset - A club with the head set behind the shaft.

Open stance - The left foot is dropped behind the imaginary line of the direction of the ball. This allows the golfer to face more in the direction the ball is going to travel.

Out of bounds - The area outside of the course in which play is prohibited. A player is penalized stroke and distance. That is he must replay the shot with a penalty of one stroke.

Overlapping grip - As used by a right-handed player having the little finger of the right hand overlapping the space between the forefinger and second finger of the left hand. The opposite for a left-handed player.

P-Q

Par - The number of strokes a player should take to complete a round with good performance. Par for each hole is given on the scorecard.

Penalty stroke - An additional stroke added to a player's score for a rules violation

Pin - Same as "flagstick"

Pin-high - A ball even with the pin but off to one side. Same as "hole high"

Pin placement (pin position) - The position of a hole on a putting green on any given day.

Pitch - A short shot lofting the ball into the air in a high arc and landing with backspin

Pitch and putt - A short golf course designed primarily for approaching and putting.

Pitch and run - The same as a pitch shot but hit with a lower-numbered club to reduce loft and backspin. This allows the ball to run after it lands on the putting green.

Pitching wedge - An iron club designed for making pitch shots

Pivot - The rotation of the shoulders, trunk and pelvis during the golf swing.

Placement - Accuracy in the targeting of a shot.

Play - To strike the ball with a club. The action of playing the game of golf.

Play off - To determine a winner in a tie match by playing further holes or a further round.

Playing through - Passing another group of players who are playing ahead

Pop up - A short, high shot.

Practice green - Green set up for putting practice.

Preferred lie - Local rules which allow a player to improve his lie in a specific manner without penalty

Pro-Am - A competition which pairs professional players with amateurs.

Pro shop - The golf course shop operated by the head professional where equipment is sold.

Provisional ball - A ball played if the previously played ball may be lost or out of bounds.

Public links - A course open to the public.

Pull - A ball that goes to the left of the target with little curve as hit by a right-handed player. The converse applies to left-handed players.

Punch - Low, controlled shot into the wind. It is made by slamming the club down into the ball with a short swing

Push - A ball that goes to the right of the target with very little or no curving for a right handed player. Or the converse for a left-handed player. As opposed to "pull"

Putt - The shot made on the putting green. From a Scottish term meaning to push gently or nudge.

Putt out - To hole the ball with a putt.

Putter - A short-shafted club with a straight face for putting.

Putting green - The surface area around the hole that is specially prepared for putting.

R

R & A - Royal and Ancient Golf Club of St. Andrews.

Reading the green - Determining the path which the ball will take on its way to the hole by analyzing the contour and texture of the green.

Regular shaft - A shaft with normal flex.

Reverse overlap - For a right-handed player, a putting grip in which the index finger of the right hand overlaps the little finger of the left and the converse for a left-handed player..

Rough - Long grass areas adjacent to fairway, greens, tee off areas or hazards.

Round - A complete game of golf - 18 holes is one round

Rub of the green - Any accident, not caused by a player or caddie, that moves or stops a ball in play and for which no relief is given under the rules. This is when your ball is deflected by agencies beyond your control that are not part of the match or the competitor's side in stroke play.

Run - The distance the ball rolls on the ground or when it lands on the ground

Run-up - An approach shot that is close to the ground or on the ground.

S

Sand trap - The common name for a bunker

Sand wedge - An iron with a heavy flange on the bottom that is used primarily to get out of sand traps.

Scoop - An improper swing in which the club has a digging or scooping action

Semi-private course - A course that has members but is still open to the public.

Set - A full set of golf clubs.

Set up - To position yourself for the address.

Shaft - The part of the club joined to the head

Shank - A shot struck by the club's hosel. Travels to the right of the intended target.

Short game - The part of the game that is made up of chip shots, pitching and putting

Short irons - The highly lofted irons.

Side - Can mean the first 9 holes (front side) or the last 9 (back side) of an 18 hole course.

Sidehill lie - A lie with the ball either above or below your feet.

Sink a putt - Make a putt.

Slice - A shot that curves strongly from left to right as a result of sidespin. The converse applies to a left-handed player.

Slope - Adjusts your handicap to the difficulty of the course you play. The more difficult the course, the more strokes you'll need. Under slope, golfers will no longer have a handicap. You will have an index. An average course will have a slope rating of 113. Your index is a mathematical calculation of your playing ability on an average course. Maximum index allowed is 36.4 for men and 40.4 for women. Conversion charts will be located at the first tee.

Sole - The bottom of the club head

Sole plate - The metal plate on the bottom of woods

Spike mark - Mark made on the green by the cleats of a golf shoe.

Spot putting - A player aims at a spot on the green that will allow the ball to roll into the cup, rather than directly at the hole.

Spring - The flexibility of the club shaft.

Square stance - Placing your feet in a line parallel to the direction you which the ball to travel

Stance - The position of your feet when addressing the ball.

Starter - Person who determines the order of play from the first tee.

Stipulated round - The playing of all holes of a course in the correct order

Straightaway - A hole having a straight fairway.

Straight-faced - Refers to a club with little or no loft on the face.

Stroke - The forward motion of the club head made with the intent to hit the ball whether contact is made or not.

Stroke play - A competition in which the total number of strokes for one round, or a pre-determined number of rounds, determines the winner.

Sudden death - When in a match or stroke competition the score is tied after completing the round, play continues until one player wins a hole

Summer rules - Ordinary play according the Rules of Golf.

Surlyn - Material from which most golf balls are made of.

Sweet spot - The dead center of the face of the club

Swing - The action of stroking the ball.

T

Takeaway - The start of the backswing

Tap in - A very short putt.

Tee - A disposable device, normally a wooden peg, on which the ball is placed for driving. Also refers to the area from which the ball is hit on the first shot of the hole. Originally a pile of sand used to elevate the ball for driving.

Tee off - To play a tee shot.

Tee up - To begin play by placing the ball on the tee.

Tee-shot - A shot played from a tee.

Teeing ground - The area in which you must tee off your ball. Ball must be teed off within the markers and no more than two club lengths behind them.

Temporary green - A green used in the winter to save the permanent green.

Three ball - Three players playing against each other with each playing their own ball.

Three-quarter shot - Less than a full shot. A shot made with a reduced swing.

Threesome - A match in which two players play the same ball and alternate strokes and play against a single player. Also means three players playing a round together.

Tight fairway - A narrow fairway.

Toe - The part of the club farthest from where in joins the shaft

Toed in - A clubhead having a specialty prominent toe with a slightly turned-in face.

Top - To hit the ball above its center causing it to roll or hop rather than rise

Topspin - The forward rotation of the ball in motion.

Touch - Accuracy, especially in putting.

Tournament - A stroke or match play competition. A competition in which a number of golfers compete.

Trajectory - The flight path of the ball.

U-V

Uncock - To straighten the wrists in the downswing.

Underclubbing - Using a club that does not give the needed distance

Unplayable lie - A lie in which the ball is impossible to play such as in a thicket of trees.

Up - A shot reaching at least as far as the hole.

Up and down - Getting out of trouble or out of a hazard and into the hole.

Upright swing - A swing that carries the club head more directly backward and upward from the ball.

W-Z

Waggle - Movement of the club head prior to swinging. A flourishing of the club behind and over the ball.

Water hole - A hole with water, such as a stream or lake, that forces the players to shoot over it

Whipping - The material used to wrap the space where the head and shaft are joined

Whippy - A shaft more flexible than normal.

Winter rules - Usually local golf rules that allow the player to improve the lie of the ball on the fairway

Wood - A club, which can be made of wood or metal, that has a large head and is used for shots requiring greater distance. Usually a numbered set of 5 or more starting with the driver and proceeding to the 5 wood

Printed in Great Britain
by Amazon.co.uk, Ltd.,
Marston Gate.